HAYES PRESS

Studies in the Book of Revelation

HAYES PRESS Christian Publisher

Contents

I

Part One

1

A PATTERN OF REVELATION (JOHN TERRELL)

Few would dispute that one of the hardest tasks before the student of the Revelation is the interpretation of the details of the many visions and images which it contains. This fact alone indicates to us the need for a wide-angled survey of this final book of Scripture, which is so enthralling but so puzzling in parts. Does it present a coherent pattern of teaching which itself might help us in grappling with some of its more detailed aspects? Can we detect a construction whose lines may circumscribe our thoughts when they might otherwise stray into the area of fanciful speculation?

Students of the Word have always marvelled at the structure of Scripture as a whole, with the remarkable correspondence between Old and New Testaments as in each the elements of divine creative work, history, prophetic teaching, and predictive prophecy unfold. Then within these (and possibly other) primary divisions of Scripture, further patterns may be discerned as in, for example, the Pentateuch or the four-fold Gospel. The whole may be likened to an examination of the physical works of God in creation, further and more detailed examination of which reveals progressively more minute wonders of order and design. Now it is, of course, into the scriptural corpus of predictive prophecy that the book of Revelation mainly fits. (We may usefully remind fellow-students at this point of the excellent "A Study in Prophetic Principles" by George Prasher Jnr, available from www.hayespress.org).

A detailed study of the distribution of predictive prophecy throughout the Scriptures offers itself as an engaging study per se; and major portions in Old and New Testaments repay study in relation to one another. Thus it is that comparative examination of the context of Revelation with that of Daniel and Ezekiel appear later in this book. Within the New Testament we can identify the end-time prophecies of the Lord Himself in Matthew 24 and Luke 21, followed by a limited excursion into this field by Paul (mainly in 1 and 2 Thessalonians), and culminating in the more detailed treatment of the subject in Revelation. In the Gospels and in the Thessalonian epistles, the standpoint of the prophecy is notably that of men and women on earth receiving instruction and warning on end-time events. In the case of the Lord's teaching, the nation of Israel is primarily the object of the teaching; and where Paul or other apostle (e.g. John in 1 Jn 2) are concerned, the saints of their day received the message as relating to themselves or their successors in the Faith.

The depiction of future events in the Revelation, however, is heaven-centred, and John finds himself taken up into the celestial realms at an early stage of his great visionary experience to observe the development of the terminal divine purpose for the earth and mankind. It is this view from the heavenly throne and sanctuary which is associated with the complexity of the visions which flow one into the other in the sequences of the seals, the trumpets and the bowls in particular. It is as though we have approached closer than ever before to the thoughts of God Himself in the detailed analysis of His motives and purposes in the final judgement of this world. The resultant imagery presents some of the most difficult problems of interpretation in all Scripture, problems which also arise in varying degree in the books of Daniel and Ezekiel.

Turning now more specifically to the main pattern of the book of Revelation we immediately think of chapter 1 verse 19 — "the things which thou sawest, and the things which are, and the things which shall come to pass hereafter." There is a wide agreement amongst students of this book that this refers firstly to the immediately preceding vision which John had experienced of the risen Lord; then to the messages given for the seven Asian churches; and thirdly to the predictive prophecies which occupy the greater part of the book (from chapter 4 onwards). Even apart from this reference itself the book immediately presents this sub-division to the most superficial reader. "The things which thou sawest" and "the things which are" are themselves intimately related, being concerned with the seven churches as lampstands of divine testimony, with the Lord of the lampstands Himself revealed in such dazzling majesty.

We cannot but pause in worship before the arresting wonder of His infinite grace in so relating Himself to these few struggling saints on earth; some beleaguered heroes; some ensnared backsliders; some lukewarm failures; all precious to Him of the flaming eyes and the voice of many waters. These things then form the first section of this Revelation of Jesus Christ. Thus is demonstrated the essential unity of God's purposes for and in the saints of this dispensation, and for the execution of His judgement upon the world in which they serve and suffer. The God who cares for and judges the saints applies the same righteous adjudication to the world, all through the glorious One presented so variously as divine Lamb, Lion, Word, Bridegroom, King of kings and Lord of lords.

Passing on to look more particularly at "the things which shall come to pass hereafter," we immediately realize that the divine dealings with the earth and its inhabitants, which occupy the remainder of the book, are themselves presented in a discernible pattern. This consists in the main of the three sequences of seven judgements as seen in the seals, trumpets and bowls, with certain events interposed between the sixth and seventh seals and trumpets. Then, between the trumpets and the bowls is placed the quite lengthy passage dealing with the vision of the woman and the dragon, Michael's conflict, the rising of the beast and of the two-horned lamb, and mount Zion of the Lamb and the 144,000 (chapters 12-14). Following the out-pouring of the bowls containing the last plagues we are led into the Armageddon narrative and the destruction of Babylon (chapters 15-19). Then the final revelation is of the conquering Word of God, the 1,000 years' binding of Satan, the final conflict, and the new heaven and new earth.

As we survey this prophetic scene broadly, we immediately face the question as to whether the narrative is truly sequential in its entirety. Clearly this is true of certain parts, notably the final section where a consummation of divine purposes is demonstrated. Then again, within the separate sequences of the seals, trumpets and bowls, a time sequence can hardly be doubted. It is, of course, with regard to these three series of judgements that a large body of expositors has pointed to an overlap or overlay of recorded events. Two matters in particular might be commented on in this connection. The first is the comparison of the details of the judgements associated with the seals, trumpets and bowls. The correspondence of individual features of first and first, second and second, etc., is often more striking in relation to the trumpets and bowls—for example in the scene of death in earth and sea connected with the second trumpet and second bowl; the mention of rivers and fountains in the third trumpet and the third bowl.

One of the most impressive elements of correspondence affects all three sequences in their final, seventh stages, i.e., the prominence of thunders, voices, lightnings, earthquakes; suggesting in each case a culminating unleashing of the power of the elements. At the same time there are also notable differences between the three judgement series, not least significantly perhaps in their smaller details, e. g., the second trumpet points to one third of sea creatures dying, while the second bowl marks the death of all marine life. (Repeated scripture references have been omitted in these comments since they can only readily be followed with the Scriptures open before one and the narrative followed in the appropriate chapters of Revelation.) What is perhaps the most compelling factor towards the overlap view of these sequences is the climax of each which seems to point clearly to the event of the coming to earth of the Son of Man (Rev.6:16; 11:15; 16:14-16).

The temptation to regard everything after chapter 11 or even after chapter 13, where the beast arises in great power, as belonging to the second half of the 70th week of Daniel is probably best resisted. It is certainly difficult to sustain. One feature which does seem significant, however, is the appearance of the temple and sanctuary (Rev.11:19) with further similar emphasis in Revelation 15:5-8 immediately preceding the pouring out of the bowls. Prior to this the standpoint would appear to have been more centred on the throne. Are the severest presentations of the divine judgements associated with God's sanctity and holiness rather than His authority and dominion? For the enemy to challenge His exclusive demand on men's obedience is one thing; their seduction in the matter of worship, another, even more solemn.

2

INTERPRETATION OF SYMBOLISM IN SCRIPTURE (LES HORNE)

It is difficult to present material on such a controversial and complex subject. In working it through I have come up with a series of statements, each one a proposition that a student can examine in the light of his own knowledge of the Scriptures. I do not expect that anyone would agree with every statement, and would be disappointed if they did. I make each one as a point for discussion.

1. Symbolism is used to communicate effectively and descriptively This may be the most startling statement of all because there is a popular view that the intention of a symbol is to interpose between reality and the seeing eye. A symbol is difficult to interpret when it is not familiar. The question is whether "seven heads and ten horns" was more familiar to a first century Christian than to a Christian today. There is evidence that it would be much more familiar to the first century believer as a form of expression and that he would respond to the phrase much more sensitively than the average Christian today. But, because symbolism is used to communicate, that does not mean that the reality is fully represented or explained by the symbol. It contains a certain degree of significance that history and further revelation may amplify.

2. Symbolism is based on simplicity and strong emotional appeal. The

emotional impact of symbols is modified by time, changing environment and translation. By simplicity I mean that the symbol represents in simple terms something that may be more complex. A child can easily picture most of the symbols of Scripture, and could draw many of them. I certainly believe that the Holy Spirit was communicating to the whole age, not only to the first readers. There are some symbols which may have a greater or different impact on us than on them. I would also suggest that there are many other ways in which the mind of God is communicated, and that we do not have to share the first century Christians' world view in its entirety to understand what the Word is saying to us.

3. It is necessary clearly to distinguish between the symbol and the reality. This, I think, is a very important statement. Usually the symbol is a representation of a particular facet of the reality. The lion, for instance, is a symbol of royalty and power, but in other instances he may represent savagery and destructive ferocity. Sometimes a figure, used in different ways, may become significant in many aspects. The lamb is an example of this, and the Lamb of Revelation has many facets, but it is still necessary not to confuse the representation with the reality it represents.

4. Fantastic symbols, composed of incongruous details, are made up of individual symbols which each have an identifiable meaning For example: Revelation 5:6 – and a Lamb standing (the Lamb of God) as though it had been slain (bearing the marks of death) with seven horns (symbols of authority, often of aggression) and seven eyes (the seven Spirits of God, His channels of perception and involvement in the activities on earth). Look at this symbol in terms of these four statements. It communicates effectively and descriptively; it is a very simple, if unusual, figure with strong emotional appeal, and each characteristic described has its separate significance.

5. Interpretation of a Scriptural symbol, unless the text provides it, requires close acquaintance with the whole book, with the way in which the writer is communicating, and with other Biblical usage of the same or similar symbols

It would be a mistake to try to understand the scarlet-coloured beast of Revelation 17:3 without an acquaintance with the whole of Revelation. It would be a mistake to interpret it without an understanding of the idiom of prophetic writing. It is useful to be aware of the general way in which the word "beast" is used in the Scriptures, that it carries a different weight from our word "animal," and that Daniel used it in a similar but possibly not identical sense as did John.

6. Because other usages of the same symbol are known it may not represent the same thing For example, the two witnesses of Zechariah 4 may not be the same two men as in Revelation 11. There are many other examples.

7. Interpretation of symbols without clear Scriptural guidance can be very misleading There are sects whose teachings rest heavily on misinterpreted symbols. The emphasis in Christian living is on experiencing and teaching truth. Too often, I believe, the debate of ideas has been an escape route from Christian action. There was a good deal of material written before 1945 on the idea that Hitler and Mussolini might be the beast and the false prophet. The energy so expended could have been put to better use.

8. The Book of Revelation has a carefully planned structure It uses numbers in a symbolic way and also groups things in numerical relationships. I am very wary of the general use of numerology, but it is quite clear that sometimes numbers are used in a symbolic way and this is particularly so in Revelation.

In conclusion then, I would suggest that it is neither possible nor desirable in our present state of knowledge to interpret every scriptural symbol. I would confine interpretation to three kinds and question the wisdom of any wider enterprise. Symbols can safely be interpreted which are:

1. Explained by the writer, e. g., Revelation 1:20; Daniel 4:9.

2. Explained in generally similar usage. The sword in Revelation 1:16, is the

same sword as in Revelation 19:75, with the latter passage providing some interpretation of the symbol. Hebrews 4:12 also uses the same figure and adds another dimension to its meaning. In fact, the figure is used a number of times, both in Old and New Testaments, but when it is used in Psalm 57:4, and Proverbs 5:4, there are very different connotations.

3. Explained by inference, supported by other scriptures. The beast is a symbol, a very forceful and simple one used to represent a world authority. When the figure is used in Daniel, it emphasizes the brutal, destructive nature of authority. In Revelation the emphasis seems to be on the aspect of God-defying, anti-Christ power. The inference that we are safe in accepting is that the Holy Spirit used the symbol of a beast on occasions to represent worldly, ungodly authority. We cannot infer that each time the symbol is used it represents the same person or the same total characteristics.

I hope that these notes may provide a basis for thought and discussion. The main emphasis in it all, and one that I have tried to make clear, is that the reality is far more important than the symbol because the reality is a living part of the purposes of God. Interpreting symbols, as was speaking in tongues, is a pointless exercise unless it is a way of coming into touch with the reality of the living God at work in this world.

3

GOD THE FATHER, AS SEEN IN THE BOOK OF REVELATION (IAN PENN)

The Father is so called by name five times in the book of Revelation. Such a comparatively small number of occurrences in a book which abounds with divine titles suggests a careful discrimination which demands close attention, especially since the relevant verses are so strikingly similar. They are:

1. He made us to be a kingdom, to be priests unto His God and Father (1:6);
2. He that overcometh, and he that keepeth My works unto the end, to him will I give authority over the nations: and he shall rule them with a rod of iron, as the vessels of the potter are broken to shivers; as I also have received of My Father (2:26,27);
3. He that overcometh shall thus be arrayed in white garments;... and I will confess his name before My Father, and before His angels (3:5);
4. He that overcometh, I will give to him to sit down with Me in My throne, as I also overcame, and sat down with My Father in His throne (3:21);
5. And I saw, and behold, the Lamb standing on the mount Zion, and with Him a hundred and forty and four thousand, having His name, and the name of His Father, written on their foreheads (14:1);

The Father is here always spoken of as the Father of the Lord Jesus Christ.

"

That is to say, God is not primarily viewed in these verses as the Creator (e. g. as in Acts 17. 29), nor as Father of children of God (as in John 1:12); nor as the Father of those children of God who, by the process of spiritual growth, display the character of Christ and are called sons of God (as in Romans 8:14; or as in the detail of 2 Cor. 6:18). The Father is viewed as the Begetter of an only and Beloved Son who is like Him in every respect, and in whom dwelleth all the fulness of the Godhead bodily. Not only do all these verses have to do with this Name but they also all concern the place of the Name. Of all the New Testament writers, the apostle John refers most frequently to "the Father" and "My Father." The purpose of his Gospel is that we might have eternal life in the Son. His epistles develop this concept in their exhortation to display this life, which is the life of the Son, in the life of the individual who thus will show true sonship. It is therefore fitting that in the Revelation John should deal with the Place where such sonship should be seen, and where the Son of God has ensamplary preeminence.

The first four references are all in the early part of the Revelation and so concern the "things which are." The last reference is more difficult to understand since it concerns "that which shall come to pass hereafter." The first four references have therefore to do with churches of God and the first of these is by way of introduction. Thus "His God and Father" relates to the Lord Jesus, firstly as the perfect Man so standing in relation to His God and secondly as the Son, Only Begotten of the Father. Just as both natures are important in salvation so too are they in service, particularly (as Hebrews demonstrates) in the matter of priestly service. The punctuation of this verse indicates (by way of contrast with Exodus 19:6) that all in churches of God (the kingdom) are priests. Thus what the Son is, in a measure the saints are too. It is particularly in this way that the verse serves as an introduction to the remainder. Obedience (to the will of the Father) is the kernel of sonship (Hebrews 5:8) and none is more obedient than the Lord Jesus Christ.

It is exactly this matter of obedience and its corollary, faithfulness, which is most prominent in these five verses in Revelation. Their meaning can thus be explained and expounded by:

1. God is faithful, through whom ye were called into the Fellowship of His Son Jesus Christ our Lord (1 Cor.1:9) and
2. Moses indeed was faithful in all God's house as a servant . . . But Christ as a Son, over God's house (Heb.3:5,6, RV margin).

These verses show the Son in His supreme likeness to the Father in the matter of faithfulness. They also show that the Fellowship belongs not simply to the Lord Jesus but to "His Son"; similarly Christ is over God's house "as a Son." In their overcoming, those mentioned in Revelation will show true likeness to Christ, true sonship, in the Place where it is meant to be shown. They are thus true sons of Zion and may be correctly likened to fine gold; gold which, like that of the Tabernacle, shines like the effulgence of His glory (Heb.1:3). (It should be noted, of course, that Hebrews 1:3 refers to the unique glory of the eternal Son).

The reward for the overcomers who show such sonship has a filial nature in that they are appointed to share that which belongs to the Son whom they have sought to emulate. Compare Rev.2:26,27 with Psalm 2:2-9, (also Matt.20:23); and Rev.3:5 with Phil.2:8-11 and the numerous verses which speak of the confession before God of the name of the Lord Jesus. The fifth reference describes men who are the firstfruits of a harvest to be reaped in a future day. We can understand something of the men's significance from what has been said above about the companion verses in the earlier part of the book. By whatever name this group will be called, in practice they will be the fellowship of His Son. They have His Name placed before them, their habitat is Mount Zion. They sing before the throne. They follow the Lamb, their Redeemer, whereever He goes. Their virginity, truthfulness and freedom from blemish are their outstanding characteristics which they must have shown in their previous earthly lives.

Virginity has no meaning without earthly existence while the absence of blemish characterizes all who dwell with Him (Rev.21:27) and so could not be considered outstanding. It would seem then that these men showed these characteristics on earth perhaps desiring to dwell with no other but Him, counterparts in a day to come of those mentioned in 1 Corinthians 7:24 and Matthew 19:12. Their reward cannot be to be His Bride, for that honour belongs to those of a preceding dispensation, but having shown true sonship and so truly proved themselves to be fit companions for the Bridegroom, they are given that position for ever.

Thus the careful reference to the Father in the book of Revelation draws attention to the importance of the truth of Sonship in relation to the Place of the Name. As He is so like the Father, so those who dwell with Him should be like Him and enter into a reward which is related to the quality of their earthly service.

4

THE LAMB, AS SEEN IN REVELATION (JOHN ARCHIBALD)

By type and simile the Son of God is described in many parts of Scripture as a Lamb. This description predominates in the Revelation. It carries the associations derived from such passages as Genesis 22:7,8, "Where is the lamb for a burnt offering? And Abraham said, God will provide Himself the lamb for a burnt offering, my son," and Isaiah 53:7, "A lamb that is led to the slaughter"; and many other portions. The original word used in the Revelation means a little lamb, which is perhaps intended to convey not only the characteristic of patient suffering but also a special ability to attract affection from the onlooker.

The Lamb as King and Lord

It is interesting to note that the Hebrew word used in the Old Testament passages already quoted means a young lamb. However, the Lamb in Revelation has Lordly attributes and a majestic presence. The title is first introduced in chapter 5, where He is announced as the Lion that is of the tribe of Judah, and John writes, "I saw in the midst of the throne and of the four living creatures, and in the midst of the elders, a Lamb standing, as though it had been slain." Jacob described Judah as a lion's whelp (Gen.49:9), but here

John beheld the majesty of the adult lion at the centre of the regal splendour of heaven. The Lamb is Lord of lords, and King of kings (Rev.17:14).

There follows in chapter 5 the account of how created ones of the most exalted heavenly rank fall down before the Lamb and sing the glorious redemption song recorded in verses 9 and 10. In chapter 6 the Lamb, having taken the book out of the right hand of Him that sat on the throne (5:7), opens the seals and with these there is associated the outpouring of divine judgement on the earth. This calls to mind the occasion in the synagogue in Nazareth when the Lord took into His hand the book of the prophet Isaiah and read to the assembly the words of grace which were that day fulfilled in their ears (Luke 4). On that day He stopped reading before the words, "and the day of vengeance of our God." The same One who proclaimed the acceptable year of the Lord in Luke 4 is seen in Revelation 6 opening the seals of the book, which initiated the fearful events indicated in this chapter.

The Lamb as Judge

In this connection we have the words of Rev.5:9, "Worthy art Thou to take the book, and to open the seals thereof; for Thou wast slain, and didst purchase unto God with Thy blood men ... " He was slain for men and therefore is particularly qualified to judge men. The Father "gave Him authority to execute judgement, because He is the Son of Man" (John 5:27). In considering this sobering aspect of the Lamb please note the expression "the wrath of the Lamb" in Rev.6:16, and also the terrible consequences for those who worship the beast and receive his mark: "He shall be tormented with fire and brimstone in the presence of the holy angels, and in the presence of the Lamb" (Rev.14:10).

The Lamb as Shepherd

By contrast there is the beautiful description of the Lamb as Shepherd in Rev.7:17, where those who come out of the great tribulation with honour are specially cared for. How tenderly the Lamb will deal with those faithful ones who have suffered so much, guiding them unto fountains of waters of life!

The Lamb as Bridegroom and Lamp

We come now to the closing chapters of the Revelation where the Lamb is seen as Bridegroom, and where we have the description of the holy city, new Jerusalem, the eternal home of the wife of the Lamb. In contemplating this glorious vision we must try to free our minds from the restricted patterns of thought acquired by experience of this fallen world. The city is from heaven (Rev.21:2,10) and is found in the new earth where all is perfection. "The building of the wall thereof was jasper: and the city was pure gold, like unto pure glass. The foundations of the wall of the city were adorned with all manner of precious stones" (Rev.21:18,19). These materials convey the idea of shining beauty, exquisite workmanship and mature excellence where there is no flaw or defect. Surely our spirits are moved when we observe that in all that scene of bright perfection there is no trace of damage save only the disfigurement implied in the words, "A Lamb standing, as though it had been slain" (Rev.5:6). The word translated "slain" implies a death of violence, nor was it unplanned or unexpected violence. In chapter Revelation 13:8 He is described as "the Lamb that hath been slain from the foundation of the world". It was the divine will that He should suffer and die, and for ever carry in His raised and glorified Person the wounds with which He was wounded for our transgressions.

We gladly note, however, that the Lamb is not on this account an object of pity in that glorious city that John saw. Indeed, "the city hath no need of the sun, neither of the moon, to shine upon it: for the glory of God did lighten it, and the lamp thereof is the Lamb" (Rev.21:23). He is the resplendent source of light and warmth in that better country. Unlike the sun which rises and sets, giving to this world day and night, His brightness is undimmed and "there shall be no night there" (Rev.21:25). It is only because of Him that the city has beauty at all. The light which flashes so brilliantly from the sparkling materials of its construction is light from Him, and even the crystal brightness of the river of water of life proceeding out of the throne is but a reflection of Him. The Lamb is all the glory Of Immanuel's land.

In conclusion, we note that His brightness is not binding to the beholder, for "His servants shall do Him service; and they shall see His face" (Rev.22:3,4). Even now God has "shined in our hearts, to give the light of knowledge of the glory of God in the face of Jesus Christ" (2 Cor.4:6).

> But if the little that we know
> Of Thee and Thine while here below
> Such triumph gives, what will it be
> When face to face Thyself we see?

5

GOD, THE HOLY SPIRIT, AS SEEN IN REVELATION (ALAN HYLAND)

The Lord Jesus taught His apostles on the night of His betrayal many things concerning the Spirit's work in them and in the world from Pentecost onwards. He also referred to the Spirit's witness to the Son, and His work in revealing to the apostles "things that are to come." He declared, "He shall not speak from Himself; but what things soever He shall hear, these shall He speak; and He shall declare unto you the things that are to come. He shall glorify Me: for He shall take of Mine, and shall declare it unto you" (Jn 16:13,14). None but the Spirit of God could fulfil this work of guiding, declaring the will of God and glorifying and revealing Christ. These facets of the Spirit's mission indicate the prominence of His work in relation to Christ Himself.

From the first reference in Scripture to the activities of the Spirit, "the Spirit of God moved upon the face of the waters" (Gen.1:2), to the last, where "the Spirit and the Bride say, Come" (Rev.22:17), He is at work, speaking and inspiring men in His sovereign activity. At the close of the first century of the Christian era, the apostle John was commissioned by God to write a book, the content of which is described as things which he saw, things which shall come to pass hereafter, truths which basically centre on the Lord Jesus Christ Himself. The book is therefore fittingly described as "the Revelation of Jesus Christ"

(Rev.1.1).

There are some eighteen references to the Spirit in the book of Revelation. Apart from the expression "the seven Spirits of God," used twice, He is called "The Spirit." The order of the greeting (1:4,5) is indicative of the inner relations of the Trinity, and is in keeping with the truth of subjection in the Godhead implied elsewhere in the New Testament. From the association of the divine Persons, the Father (Him which is and which was and which is to come) and Jesus Christ, it is clear that the term "the seven Spirits of God" must be interpreted as referring to the Person of the Holy Spirit. The seven Spirits would teach the full deity and perfection of His Person. The seven lamps which are before the throne, representing the seven Spirits of God, reveal the work of the Spirit in the full knowledge and perfect rule of that throne in the whole universe, as well as indicating its rule over those gathered in the seven churches. In each of the letters to the seven churches in Asia the voice of the Spirit in the words, "He that hath an ear, let him hear what the Spirit saith to the churches," is identified with the voice of Christ.

The messages to the churches individually and to all of these together, have a Spirit-given application to all, and indeed to churches of God in our time. The presentation of Christ to each church is relevant to its individual position and condition and even in His several names there is comfort and hope. To the overcomers there are promises and rewards, which will be perfectly just and suitable for the recipients. The Holy Spirit Himself will apply to churches of God the principles and truths He reveals to those seven golden lampstands. Though the record of errors, failures and successes of those early churches had a particular application to them, the letters are like a mirror in which we can see ourselves in churches of God today. As to them so to us, the word is, "He that hath an ear, let him hear what the Spirit saith to the churches."

The fact that there were seven churches addressed and that He had a different message for each is a further indication of His sovereign activity in the sphere of God's rule among His people gathered in assemblies of God. The expression,

"I was in the Spirit" (1:10; 4:2), seems to indicate special experiences that John had to enable him to appreciate the nature of his mission, to see the glory of the Lord and the majesty and grandeur of scenes in heaven. It is part of the Spirit's work to take up men, revealing in them, to them and through them in His sovereign control the historic and prophetic content of the word of God. It was through the Spirit's activity that John was able to record the book of Revelation. At the close of Revelation, and therefore of the New Testament, we have that incomparable promise of Christ, "Yea; I come quickly", and coupled with it the final invitation, "the Spirit and the Bride say come." The response of all whose hearts are illuminated by the Spirit's testimony is fittingly expressed among the closing words of Scripture: "Amen: come, Lord Jesus" (Rev.22:20).

> For Christ, my Master's quick return,
> 'Tis He who teaches me to yearn;
> The Paraclete, who, wondrous grace!
> Makes my poor heart His dwelling place.
> (C. M. Luxmoore)

6

SOME TITLES OF THE LORD IN REVELATION (ERIC ARCHIBALD AND MARTIN ARCHIBALD)

The Alpha and the Omega

In these letters which come first and last respectively in the Greek alphabet the Almighty makes known His eternal character within the compass of human language. God graciously interposed in our lives when He shined in our hearts by the power of His word (2 Cor.4.6), and made the beginning of a new creation (2 Cor.5:17). Three times the Spirit caused John to pen the words, "I am the Alpha and the Omega" (Rev. 1:8; 21:6; 22:13), thus expressing the perfection of the Word of God. "I am the first, and I am the last … ye are My witnesses," God said to Israel (Is.44:6-8), and this was their responsibility as having received the oracles of God. Within the breastplate of judgement Moses placed not only the Lights but also the Perfections (Lev.8:8, which is the middle verse of the Torah). Yet if the perfection of the Law found no answering perfection in the lives of Israelites, the word of faith still directs the heart to Christ as the end of the Law unto righteousness to everyone that believeth (Rom. 10:4).

Last among the verses which begin with the letter Tau in Ps.119 is the confession, "I have gone astray like a lost sheep; seek Thy servant" (v.176). As head of the body, the Church, He is the beginning (Col.1:18,19) and the fulness (Eph.1:23). Jesus Christ is the same yesterday and today, yea and for ever (Heb.13:8). We know that it is God's purpose to sum up all things in Christ (Eph.1:10), for He is before all things and in Him all things consist (Col.1:17). When Babylon threatened to overthrow Israel, Jehovah reminded them, "I am the first, I also am the last" (Is.48:12). Thus God declares the end from the beginning (Is.46:10). The fact that He is the former of all things makes the portion of His worshippers distinctive (Jer.10:16). He has promised that to him that is athirst He will give of the fountain of the water of life freely (Rev.21:6). In the days of His flesh the Lord said, "Heaven and earth shall pass away: but My words shall not pass away (Lk.21:33).

The One who was still the God of Abraham in the day when He made Himself known to Moses as the "I am" (see Jn 8:58) has brought life and incorruption to light through the gospel (2 Tim.1:10). Whatever the reward for each man's work when He returns, the hymn strikes a note of trust and affection:

'Tis Jesus, the First and the Last,
Whose Spirit shall guide us safe home;
We'll praise Him for all that is past,
And trust Him for all that's to come.

The Amen

The Amen was used when one confirmed the word of another. Jeremiah, while condemning Hananiah for making the people to trust in a lie, said Amen to the part of the prophecy which dealt with the return of the vessels of the Lord's house (Jer.28:6). Another example of its use is where all the people had to confirm the curse upon idolatry by saying Amen (Deut.27:75). The word expressed a commitment with regard to the truth of what had been said or spoken. God would hear and witness the saying of Amen. It is used at all the divisions between the books of the Psalms, perhaps with the thought of participation in the praises, prayers and thanksgivings in them. In the New Testament is is also associated with thanksgiving (1 Cor.14:16). It appears many times in the epistles of Paul to confirm a blessing, and it is to be found also in the writings of Peter and Jude (2 Pet.3:18; Jude v.25). While the saying of Amen implies a person's agreement with what is said, the authority for the fulfilment of the word of blessing lies with God. Thus Jeremiah answered and said, "Amen, O Lord" (Jer.11:5). The purpose of God who made the promises will alone accomplish them (2 Cor.1:20).

Paul the Apostle wrote to the Corinthians, "God is faithful, through whom ye were called into the fellowship of His Son Jesus Christ our Lord (1 Cor.1.9). There can only be failure for those who strive for blessing apart from the God of the Amen (Is.65:16). Even when trustworthiness is lacking among men, the Lord is a true and faithful witness (Jer.42:5). The word Amen in Hebrew signifies what is trustworthy, what one can lean upon. Moses, who was faithful in all God's house as a servant, felt the burden of Israel leaning upon him as a nursing father (Heb. "omen", Num.11:12; in the Septuagint Version 'paidagogos' or tutor). Even earlier at Rephidim (Ex.17:12) with the help of Aaron and Hur the two hands of Moses were steady (emunah) until the going down of the sun. The Hebrew words for faithfulness and for believing are from the same root. It was this quality of faithfulness which characterised the life of Daniel, when his enemies tried to find occasion against the law of his God (Dan.6:5).

From the same root also is the word "master-workman" (amon). In His character of Wisdom, the Lord was a master-workman in the beginning (Prov.8:30). The marvel of God's love is that He hath spoken unto us in His Son, His true witness on earth. He it was who walked amid the lampstands, and His speaking to the Church in Laodicea continued to express God's unbounded love and the immensity of His faithfulness (Rev.3:14).

"Son of Man"

The expression "son of man" in its simplest use in Scripture means "human being", as opposed to other orders of creation, or a person divine, as we see in Is.56:1,2: "Keep ye judgement, and do righteousness … Blessed is the man that doeth this, and the son of man that holdeth fast by it." The term acquires a lowly, insignificant note, when Balaam says "God is not a man, that He should lie; neither the son of man, that He should repent" (Num.23:19), or the poet asks "LORD, what is man, that Thou takest knowledge of him? Or the son of man, that Thou makest account of him?" (Ps.144:3) or Bildad exclaims "How much less man, that is a worm! And the son of man, which is a worm!" (Job 25:6). But when the Son of God took the form of a servant and in grace called Himself the Son of Man, He made these words a title that recalls for us both the dignity of man seen in his full spiritual stature, and at the same time the place of rejection that the Perfect Man was given by His people.

Note how the contrast between the sinful nature of our race as Balaam, the psalmist and Bildad knew it, and man as he becomes when he finds favour in sight of God, is set forth in Genesis 4. Eve said at first in her early hope, "I have gotten a man with the help of the LORD," but after the sad experience of what man's begetting brought she said, "God hath appointed me another seed instead of Abel; for Cain slew him." The salutation of the prophet as "son of man," in Daniel and many times in Ezekiel, gives the expression a further significance, as describing a messenger suited for communication with men because of his kinship with them; and when one like unto a son of man enters Daniel's vision of thrones being placed and the ancient of days, it seems remarkable to the beholder, in Dan.7:13, that someone having human form should come so near before the thronesitter, till it is realised that this Son of Man is most worthy of dominion, glory and a kingdom.

The glory of His Father will be seen by every eye when the greatest Messenger to men comes in divine power, attended by the angels that belong to Him, and renders to every man according to their deeds (Matt.16:27), with "authority to execute judgements, because he is the Son of Man" (John 5:27). As the sign of the clouds is linked in Daniel 7:13 with the likeness of a son of man, so the Lord Jesus according to His own word will return to earth "on the clouds of heaven" (Matt.26:64)— two features of the Son's coming that will also be granted to His servant the first angel sent forth with sickle to reap the harvest of the earth, so that John saw (Rev.14:14) "a white cloud; and on the cloud ... one sitting like unto a son of man."

These themes, which we have suggested are evoked by the words "son of man" may be found together in the manner of the Lord's appearing to His servant John, being especially impressed upon us in the detail of Revelation 7:13-16. The perfect humanity of the One who tabernacled amongst men is recalled in the brilliance of His countenance and the garment that clothes Him down to the foot; from His mouth that made faithful witness to men comes the power of a voice as of many waters and the sword of His Word; and this person, whose head, hair, eyes and feet are resplendent in purity, is the same Jesus, once rejected of men, who is ordained to be their judge.

"The Bright, the Morning Star"

The star of Revelation 22:16 is described by a word which before New Testament times meant "early in the day" or "of the dawn", and came also to mean "early" in general. The morning star is also referred to as the day-star (literally "light-bringer"), both terms being used in antiquity of any star or planet prominent in the Eastern sky just before dawn. So Peter contrasts the lamp "shining in a dark place", which is the word of prophecy (2 Pet.7:19), with the day-star, which is the Lord, the Word Himself, showing that when the bringer of light shall be manifested, He will draw so near to us as to arise in our hearts, as the shadows flee away and we apprehend the glorious substance, no longer knowing in part, but even as also we have been known.

To John it is given to reveal the title "the bright, the morning star", which portrays the Lord as our sure hope of an early dawn-—our meeting together with Him, before the great and terrible day. Whereas His coming as Son of Man is with the clouds, swift and sudden, the vision that He leaves with us at the end of the Omega-book of His revelation, when we have read of constellations deflected from their courses, depicts Him as a steady, unmoved hope, like the faithful witness in the sky to which Ps.89:37 compares the security of God's covenant with David and his seed. Thus the Creator, whose laying of earth's foundation made the stars of dawn sing together, expresses Himself in the qualities of things created; and He who is David's Lord yet was willing in emptying Himself to become David's son (Rev.22:16).

His birth on earth was marked by His star in the east; we shall have at His return for us a heavenly sign indeed to answer the signs of the times that the Master called us to discern. Now the Word of Truth, whose name is Jesus and who has sent His angel to testify these things for the churches, offers in Rev.2:28 to him that overcomes amidst the foul prophecy of Jezebel, nothing less than something shining clear and bright like Himself—the morning star, that surely speaks of truth pure as the fire-flaming eyes of the rewarder.

7

THE AUTHOR OF REVELATION - JOHN THE APOSTLE (JOHN BAIRD)

Of the early years of John the apostle the Scriptures furnish no definite information, but we know that he and his brother James were sons of Zebedee, a fisherman on the sea of Galilee; and that before the Lord called them they worked with their father as fishermen (Mk.1:16-20). Zebedee had hired servants, and so was apparently sufficiently prosperous to engage labour. Also, the standing of the family may be indicated by the fact that John was known to the high priest (Jn 18:15). These considerations suggest that John was brought up in a fairly prosperous family in comfortable circumstances.

John's mother would appear to have been a disciple of the Lord Jesus, for she asked that the Lord should command that "these my two sons may sit, one on Thy right hand, and one on Thy left hand, in Thy kingdom" (Matt.20:20-23). She was ambitious that her sons should advance in spiritual things and be prominently placed in the kingdom. However injudicious her request may have been, she must, at least, be credited with godly concern for those near to her by natural ties. To that extent she is worthy of commendation: we today ought to be much concerned about the spiritual progress of our younger ones in the churches of God. Comparison of Matt.27:56 with Mk 15:40 and 16:1 would suggest that Salome, one of the women that loved the Lord Jesus and ministered to Him, was the mother of John, and, if John 19:25 refers to four women, she may well have been the sister of Mary the mother of the Lord. If this reading of these scriptures is sound, John may well have enjoyed the love of the Lord Jesus for some considerable time before he was called to discipleship.

John is commonly taken to have been a mild and gentle person, but it is not without significance that the Lord called James and John "sons of thunder" (Mk 3:17). With this we should associate the fact that John was one of those who sought to silence one who cast out demons in the Lord's name but did not follow with them (Lk.9:49). John, further, was one of those who spoke of calling down fire from heaven to consume the inhospitable Samaritans (Lk.9:51–56). There was then an impetuous and severe trait in John's character, at least in his earlier years. But when we examine John's writings, he appears to us as a man of loving disposition and who rejoiced in the love of his Lord, an unmistakeable evidence that John's character was much mellowed by his close walk with the Lord.

It is reckoned that John lived to a very ripe old age; even so, the dates commonly advanced as the probable time of his death suggest that he was called to discipleship as a very young man (perhaps a little over twenty years of age). If Acts 1:21–22 is a statement of necessary qualifications for apostleship, then John must have been baptized by John the Baptist, and would be one of those awaiting the coming of the Christ; hence his readiness to follow at once when John the Baptist said, "Behold, the Lamb of God" (Jn 1:35–40). We know that Andrew was one of the two of John's disciples who followed Jesus on that day (Jn 1:40), and there can be little doubt that John was the other, for it is characteristic of John that he avoids specifically naming himself, preferring to use such terms as "another disciple" and "the disciple whom Jesus loved."

John's formal call to discipleship was later (Mk.1:19–20), and is an instance of what the Lord said about the Good Shepherd, for there we see the Good Shepherd calling His sheep by name, and the sheep, knowing the Voice, followed the Shepherd (Jn 10). Soon after John's call to apostleship (Mk.3:77), the outstanding place among the apostles that was to be his became apparent. He is, on certain occasions, seen as one of three to whom the Lord gave prominent place. With Peter and James he witnessed the raising of Jairus's daughter (Mk.5:37), the transfiguration of the Lord (Mk.9:2) and the agony of the Lord in Gethsemane (Matt.26:37; Mk.14:33). As one of the favoured four (Andrew being the fourth) he was present when the Lord prophesied on the mount of Olives (Mk.13:3-8). As one of two, Peter and himself, John followed the Lord Jesus to the house of Caiaphas after the betrayal (Jn 18:75), and was therefore a witness of at least some of the indignities suffered by the Lord at the hands of the Jews and Romans.

The same two, on hearing from Mary Magdalene, ran to the tomb and found it empty, and thus were among the first to learn the good news that the Lord was risen indeed (Lk.24:34). Peter and John are again seen acting together in the healing of the lame man and in suffering the consequent persecution (Acts 3 and 4). We note too that they were later sent to Samaria to further the work of the Lord there (Acts 8:14-25). There is no need further to multiply instances; but we should observe that, as can be seen in such passages as these and Acts 15 and Galatians 2:1-10, the position of these outstanding men amongst the apostles did not change after the Lord had ascended to the Father (though it should be observed that in the last two references James is the Lord's brother, not the son of Zebedee).

During the days of His presence the Lord had made clear indication of His chosen vessels and their special responsibilities, and after the Lord was taken up the Lord's choice was honoured among the saints. We do well to follow that pattern. If it is shown that a man is called and fitted of God for responsible service in His house, we should recognize the work of the Lord the Spirit in that man and do all in our power to facilitate his work for God.

God has given us through John a considerable portion of the New Testament, consisting of the Gospel that bears his name, three brief epistles and the

There were those who tried to impose upon the Christians those things which belonged to the Law. This was done to the Colossians but Paul advised them in the Holy Spirit: "Let no man therefore judge you in meat, or in drink, or in respect of a feast day or a new moon or a sabbath day: which are a shadow of the things to come" (Col.2:16-17). Now we have been discharged from the Law, having died to that wherein we were held (Rom.7:6). Some try to circumvent these Scriptures by drawing an artificial distinction between 'moral' and 'ceremonial' law but the Word of God makes no such distinction. It was a 'whole law' (Gal.5:3). "The bond written in ordinances" (Col.2:14) is the law and it is now blotted out for the believer, having been taken out of the way by the cross.

We cannot cover here the significance of the first day of the week but it was foreshadowed in the Old Testament (e.g. Lev.23:16). Nor have we space to speak of that sabbath rest described in Hebrews chapters 3 and 4 which remains for the people of God. That has to do with 'another day' (Heb.4:8) which is an ever present 'today', not a repetitive seventh day of 24 hours, and it is associated with God's house (Heb.3:6; Is.66:1) not with heaven as the believer's future home.

Most significantly, those who promote the sabbath observance are in proven error upon other matters of vital Biblical teaching. May we rightly divide the Word of God and prove the things that differ (2 Tim.2:15).

Revelation. The second and third epistles are very brief personal letters to fellow-believers with whom John shared a loving concern for the spiritual welfare and progress of others. The first epistle is general in character and longer than the others; like them, it is in harmony with John's Gospel. They are all palpably by the same writer, obviously a man well acquainted with the Old Testament Scriptures (Hebrew version rather than Septuagint), and having an intimate knowledge of Jerusalem and of the Holy Land. Consequently, though his Gospel consists largely of the Lord's discourses, the presentation remains graphic. A like principle applies to our preaching of the gospel today: it will gain much in every way if we have a full knowledge of the Scriptures and a clear vision of the cross of Christ. In his Gospel and his three epistles John appears to be a single-minded believer in God and His Christ.

As led of the Spirit he uses the simplest of language to express some of the most profound teachings of the Scriptures, and the reader gathers the distinct impression that the writer has accepted these deep things with all the simplicity of a child in its unquestioning trust in its parents. This tone of high faith is seen too in the Revelation, which provides the little that we know from Scripture of the end of John's life. By the time the Revelation was shown to him, he was an aged man, of high standing in the churches of God, suffering persecution and bonds for the testimony of Jesus (Rev:1:9). But prison bonds cannot hinder divine revelation, and so there was delivered that wonderful message for the seven churches in the Roman province of Asia and for us today. Such then was John the apostle; a man fitted of the Lord to bear outstanding responsibility among God's people, a man to whose care the dying Lord could trust His beloved mother (Jn 19:27), a man happy to call himself in truth "the disciple whom Jesus loved."

8

EZEKIEL AND REVELATION – A COMPARATIVE STUDY (ERIC ARCHIBALD)

Whereas the Book of the Revelation is a continuous series of visions following the message to the seven churches, the book of Ezekiel contains prophecies given at various times; and much of the book of Ezekiel is concerned with warnings about the fall of Jerusalem as the inevitable consequence of the people's behaviour. John had to write in a book what he saw and heard. Ezekiel, however, was charged to speak to the house of Israel with the Lord's words (3:4). By his actions also he was made to be a sign to the people, symbolizing by his removal, for instance, the captivity which was then imminent (12:11), and making predictions, such as the blinding of Zedekiah (12:12), which had their fulfilment in his own day (2 Kin.25:7).

While the downfall of Jerusalem was certain (12:25), Ezekiel proclaimed a message of hope for an obedient remnant (11:16). Some principles in his prophecy have their application today, as for example that of judgement beginning from the sanctuary (9:6). The inference from this order of judgement in 1 Pet.4:17 is of far-reaching significance. Such principles transcending the historical crisis of Ezekiel's own day have a bearing on the Revelation of Jesus Christ, signified by God's angel to His servant John. Since the prophet and the apostle were both granted visions of divine things, the human language which they use to describe them shows a marked resemblance, and the ways in which they were involved in the heavenly scene have their similarities.

The number of living creatures (Ezek.1:5) was four, as in Rev.4:6-8. Their characteristics expressed the One whom they served. As to their feet, they sparkled like the colour of burnished brass (Ezek.1:7), and the noise of their wings was like the voice of the Almighty, like the noise of great waters (Ezek.1:24). As the glassy sea (Rev.4:6) was like unto crystal, so Ezekiel saw the likeness of a firmament like the colour of the terrible crystal (1:22). The living creatures of Rev.4:6 were full of eyes, and so was the living creature which Ezekiel saw under the God of Israel (Ezek.10:12,20). There was a rainbow round about the throne in Rev.4:3, and Ezekiel likens the brightness round about to the bow that is in the cloud in the day of rain. It was the glory of the Lord which caused Ezekiel to fall upon his face (Ezek.1:28) even as John also did (Rev.1:17). At the time when Ezekiel was being instructed to speak to the house of Israel (3:1), he was caused to eat a book containing lamentations and mourning and woe. John also was told to eat a little book (Rev.10:9).

In both cases the book proved to be as honey for sweetness in the mouth. Ezekiel's roll was written within and without (2:10), but in Revelation 5:1 it is the book in the hand of Him that sat on the throne which is so described. After Ezekiel had eaten the roll of a book, he heard behind him the voice of a great rushing, which he attributes to the wings of the living creatures and the noise of their wheels. He heard the voice saying "Blessed be the glory of the LORD from His place." God's standard was unaltered. The court of the temple had already ceased to be a fit place for His glory. So John also (Rev.11:1) was instructed in the patience of God to measure the temple and the altar but not the court. The temple of God which John had to measure was a temple on earth. With the divine standard he had also to take the measure of the worshippers.

In 8:3 Ezekiel is lifted up and brought to see the image of jealousy set up at the gates of the inner court at Jerusalem. The Lord God had said, "They shall profane My secret place" (Ezek.7:22), and "Behold, I will profane My sanctuary" (24:21). This is the result of their whoredom with the great harlot (Ezek.16; Rev.17). In 2 Chron.36:13 we are told that Zedekiah rebelled against king Nebuchadnezzar, who had made him swear by God; so that God gave them all into his hand. And they burned the house of God. Zedekiah had despised the oath by breaking the covenant (Ezek.17:18). So that in Ezekiel 21:14 we read that "It is the sword of the great one that is deadly wounded, which entereth into their chambers."

Zedekiah's action was the undoing not only of Jerusalem but also of himself. Then the word came, "And thou, O deadly wounded wicked one, the prince of Israel, whose day is come, in the time of the iniquity of the end ... Remove the mitre" (21:25-26). But God overturned the schemes of the Babylonian. God's purpose was to establish the true succession to the throne of David. From Jeconiah would spring the tender One (Ezek.17:22), who would be a goodly cedar. The prophet looked forward to the time when this One should come who had the right to the crown. "And," said the Lord, "I will give it Him" (Ezek.21:27).

Concerning Babylon the great, John heard a voice from heaven, saying, "Come forth, My people, out of her, that ye have no fellowship with her sins" (Rev.18:4). The second beast of Revelation 13 deceiveth them that dwell on the earth, saying that they should make an image to the beast who hath the stroke of the sword and lived. This first beast whose death stroke is healed receives the worship of all on earth whose names have not been written in the book of life of the Lamb. The tabernacle of God, even them that dwell in the heaven, is out of his reach. Nevertheless he utters blasphemies against it. This deadly wounded beast makes a firm covenant, prematurely terminated by abominations, then claims the diadem to which he has no right. His image standing in the holy place, the time is ripe for the sharpened sword of Him that sat upon the horse (Rev.19:21).

The words "He that heareth, let him hear," were spoken to Ezekiel (3:27). This message is repeated to the seven churches in Rev.2.5, and also in Rev.13:9. Here attention is directed to the Lamb that hath been slain from the foundation of the world. The colossal structure of Gentile dominion will disintegrate because at its basis there is failure to acknowledge that the heavens do rule. It cannot but give way to the kingdom whose foundation is utterly trustworthy. The foundation of spiritual world-order has required the death of the Sin-bearer. He alone can uphold the righteousness of Jehovah. "I sought for a man among them," God said, "but I found none" (Ezek.22:30). In Ezek.9:4 the Lord bids the destroyers to set a mark upon the foreheads of the men that sigh because of all the abominations done in the midst of Jerusalem. See also in Revelation 7:3 the four angels are stayed from hurting the earth the seas and trees, until the servants of God are sealed on their foreheads. These are the 144,000 of Israel.

The locusts at the time of the fifth trumpet, which torment men for five months, will be powerless to hurt those who are sealed (Rev.9:5). The sword would cut down Jerusalem, and scales would determine which were for famine, which for slaughter, and which for scattering (Ezek.5:72). The second, third and fourth seals of Revelation 6 bring bloodshed, famine and death upon the earth. At the opening of the fifth seal comes the cry of the souls of the slain for vengeance (Rev.6:10). The response to the angel of the third bowl is in the same spirit (Rev.16:7). Before the sounding of the first trumpet (Rev.8:5), an angel fills a censer with the fire of the altar, adding it to the prayers of the saints, and casts the fire upon the earth. The man clothed in linen (Ezek.10:2) was to receive coals of fire from between the cherubim and scatter them over the city. Noah, Daniel and Job would not save it from the four ensuing judgements (Ezek.14:21). The words ascribed to Israel (Ezek.20:32), "We will be as the nations ... to serve wood and stone." were to bring down the fury of His judgement on them.

So the second woe of Revelation 9:20 leaves mankind unrepentant in their worship of idols. They unite with the kingdom of the beast to blaspheme the God of heaven (Rev.16:2). The attitude of the prince of Tyre in Ezekiel 28:2

is like that of the beast, and the merchandise described in Ezekiel 27 is like that of Babylon (Rev.18). Ezekiel 30:5 envisages a time when the day of the Lord is near; the time of the heathen when the league with Egypt will end in the sword. Egypt will be a prey to the fowls of the heaven, and her fall will be associated with darkened heavens (Ezek.32:4,7). The defeat of Gog is accompanied by a great shaking in the land of Israel (Ezek.38:19), though perhaps the prophet also sees that their ultimate fate is to be devoured by fire (Rev.20:9). In the scene which introduces the seven trumpets, we are told of an earthquake following the casting of fire upon the earth (Rev.8:5). The pouring out of the seventh bowl (Rev.16:18) is marked by such an earthquake.

The sixth seal is also associated with shaking of the earth, and great distur-bances follow on the shaking of the heavens. The flesh of the slain will be given to the birds at the great supper of God (Ezek.39:17; Rev.19:17). Then comes the revival and restoration of Israel foretold in the vision of dry bones (Ezek.37:24). The tabernacle of God, which the beast sought to assail with his blasphemies, will also be with them (Ezek.37:27; Rev.21:3). As in Rev.21:12,13 the gates of the city are named after the tribes of Israel, so are those in Ezekiel (48:31), even the names of the tribes being given. In Rev.21:3 we read that "God Himself shall be with them." Henceforth, Ezekiel is told, the name of the city shall be "The Lord is there." The site whereupon Ezekiel saw the frame of a city (Ezek.40:2) was on a very high mountain. Moreover the vantage point from which John saw the holy city was a mountain great and high (Rev.21:10).

9

DANIEL AND REVELATION – A COMPARATIVE STUDY (ALAN SANDS)

Our subject concerns "the theology of power." Both Daniel and Revelation proclaim the sovereignty of God: "the Most High ruleth in the kingdom of men" (Dan.4:25), and "the Lord our God, the Almighty, reigneth" (Rev.19:6). A summary of salient features follows.

1. Authors. Daniel, a Hebrew saint exiled in Babylon under two oppressive empires, searching the Scriptures and awaiting the fulfilment of God's promises (Dan.9:2). John, an aged Hebrew Christian (presumably the apostle) exiled in Patmos under a later oppressor; undoubtedly a student of Daniel (with much to say about Babylon) and awaiting the promised One (Rev.22:20).

2. Composition and prophetic outline. Both books treat of contemporary situations as well as being apocalyptic. Daniel's first six chapters include experiences of himself and his contemporaries, and the first three chapters of Revelation concern the condition of seven churches. The latter part of Daniel and virtually the entire Revelation contain visions and interpretations (and "dreams" in Daniel). Their extensive symbolism has many common features. Daniel predicts (a) things now history; e. g. world empires affecting God's people till their rejection of Messiah; and (b) things pertaining to "the time of the end" (Dan. 12:4), namely, ultimate evil leadership and the conquering kingdom of God.

Similarly, John writes of things he saw and "the things which are, and the things which shall come to pass hereafter" (Rev.1:19). The "hereafter" certainly enlarges on (b) above, but no doubt intervening history is to some extent predicted. Coming events often cast their shadows before, and some prophecies have a prior application.

A striking feature of Revelation is the frequent use of 7 (symbol of completeness). There are: 7 churches (1:11), 7 lampstands (1:12), 7 stars (1:16), 7 spirits of God (4:5), 7 seals (5:1), 7 angels (8:2), 7 trumpets (8:2), 7 thunders (10:3), 7 plagues (15:6), 7 bowls (15:7), and 7 heads (13:1). There are also seven significant signs in chapters 12 to 14. In contrast, Daniel has only two such occurrences: "seven times" (Dan.4:16), and "seventy weeks (sevens)" (9:24-26). The revelations to both Daniel and John were in a sense partial, but in the case of the latter God concluded His written revelation, and the numerous sevens stress this completeness.

3. Recipients. Daniel's use of languages additional to Hebrew, and the content of his writings, indicate that he was to some extent addressing Gentiles. For some unknown reason he did not return with the Remnant, and although he does not say so, his message was intended for future generations of God's people also. John on the other hand clearly was writing to his contemporaries in the seven churches (1:11; 22:16).

4. Purpose. A paramount objective of both books is to throw essential light on the future. Daniel says, "there is a God ... that revealeth secrets, and He hath made known ... what shall be in the latter days" (Dan.2:28). Similarly John writes of "the things which must shortly come to pass" (Rev.1:1) "hereafter" (1:19). Daniel reveals the immediate future to Gentile monarchs, to influence their behaviour, and also the distant future, principally to influence God's people, who would soon be released from Gentile captivity. John writes to

Christians living in the prospect of enforced Caesar-worship. He reveals the ultimate outcome of current trends to encourage them to overcome. The Spirit has miraculously designed the Revelation so that it is meaningful to all generations of those who seek to serve God (Rev.1:1).

5. Conclusions. The two books close on an interesting note of both contrast and comparison. Daniel's prophecy is "sealed" (whatever this may mean) "till the time of the end" (12:9). In contrast John is told "seal not up the words of the prophecy of this book; for the time is at hand" (Rev.22:10). However, both predict the same inevitable division of humanity between those who purify themselves and those who do wickedly (Dan.12:10), that is, the "righteous" and the "unrighteous" (Rev.22:11).

6. Some specific parallels. Space only permits brief consideration of some remarkable parallels:

(i) Beasts. The lion, bear, leopard, and ten-horned monster of Daniel 7 are all represented in the composite beast of Revelation 13. Is Daniel 7 concerned with the same four Gentile powers as are depicted in the image of Daniel 2? The popular affirmation of this view presents difficulties. For example, Daniel 7 concerns "four kings which shall arise" (v.17). Babylon, the first power of chapter 2 had already seen the rise of its last king when the vision was given (Dan.7:1). Another difficulty arises in verse 12 in that the lives of three beasts are prolonged. The difficulty is resolved for those who discern here a reference to a probable continuance into the end times of features of the three former powers. However as the features of all four powers appear simultaneously in the first beast of Rev.13 is it not possible that both this vision and that of Daniel 7 have their fulfilment in co-existing Gentile powers of the end time (we see features now) and an application in previous powers? [See editors' Comment A].

(ii) Ten Toes and Ten Horns. Undoubtedly the ten toes of Daniel 2, and the ten horns of Daniel 7 and Revelation 13 refer to the same Gentile powers prevailing in the end times (Dan.2:40-42; Rev.17:12,13). Is "ten" symbolic of the aggregate of world powers, or literal in respect of a ten-nation super-power? If the former, then the iron and clay of the toes might indicate totalitarian states (e.g. communistic), and other weaker democratic states. If the latter, then one such superpower is already being formed in Europe, and students of the "revived Roman Empire" view will closely follow the performance of the Treaty of Rome [See editors' Comment B]. Others might consider that in the context of Daniel's prophecies we are concerned with powers prevailing over the Holy City, and that historically Rome was succeeded by the Muslim world in this respect. A ten-nation union of Arab states is therefore suggested by some as being envisaged [See editors' Comment C].

(iii) Antichrist. The domination of the coming Ten by absolute evil incarnate, with fearful global consequences, is clearly foretold by Daniel and John. Daniel's detailed predictions of Antiochus Epiphanes, the archtype of the Antichrist (Dan.8 and 11), have undoubtedly a measure of dual application, and in fact develop into portraits of Antichrist himself, as evidenced by reference to "the time of the end" (Dan.11:55), and by John's corroboration. The "little horn" of Daniel 7, the "coming prince" of chapter 9, and the beast of Revelation 13 portray him further.

Comparing Daniel and Revelation the following features of Antichrist are confirmed:

1. His thoroughly Satanic power (Dan.8:24; 11:39; Rev.13:2),
2. His blatant blasphemy (Dan.7:25; 11:36; Rev.13:6),
3. His deadly deception (Dan.8:25; Rev.13:3,4, 12-14),
4. His total economic control (Dan.11:43; Rev.13:16,17),
5. His unprecedented persecution of Israel (Dan.7:21,25; 8:24; Rev.13:7),
6. His confrontation with Christ (Dan.8:25; Rev.17:14), and
7. His eternal destruction by Christ (Dan.7:11,26; 8:25; 11:45; Rev.19:20; 20:10).

(iv) The Great Tribulation Period. Antichrist's breaking of his seven-year treaty midway (Dan.9:27) commences the three and a half year Tribulation, the duration of which is strikingly confirmed in Daniel and Revelation. It is variously stated in terms of (a) times, (b) months, and (c) days, as indicated below.

(a) The expression "time, times and half a time" denotes the period Antichrist persecutes the saints (Dan.7:25), the time of unprecedented trouble (12:7), and the period during which those who flee are sustained (Rev.12:14).

(b) The period of 42 months refers to the siege of Jerusalem (Rev.11:2), and the Beast's reign (Rev.13:5).

(c) The 1,260 days of Rev.12:6 refer to the same period as in ch.12:14. The period during which God's witnesses prophesy is also described as 1260 days (11:3), although belonging to the first half of Daniel's 70th week. Daniel 12:11,12 mentions 1,290 days and 1,335 days, presumably in the above context of the second half of the "week.". Possibly the excess of 30 days in the former relates to the period of Israel's post-Tribulation repentance, and the further 45 days excess in the latter perhaps concludes the period of Messiah's wrath when the faithful and repentant return to be "blessed."

6. Some specific parallels (continued)

(v) Christ—His Advents. The Incarnation, in relation to both Israel and the nations, and also to Satanic opposition, is depicted in Revelation 12 in the birth of the Man Child. In contrast, Daniel's sole reference to Christ's first advent is his remarkably chronological prediction of the anointed One's shameful death, "having nothing" (Dan.9:26). In this respect however, John denotes the magnificence of the Lamb's death in terms of redemption and heavenly worship (Rev.5:9). Christ's second advent is dramatically illustrated in Daniel by the stone "cut out without hands" (Dan.2:45). The manner of His appearing is indicated: "... with the clouds of heaven ... like unto a son of man" (Dan.7:13).

John uses remarkably similar language and describes Christ sitting on the cloud (Rev.1:7; 14:14).

At His coming many millions attend Him, and one consequence is that judgement is "given to the saints" (Dan.7:10,22; Rev.20:4). John describes Him coming on a white horse with heavenly armies following (Rev.19:14), and records His promise to overcoming saints: "authority over the nations" (Rev.2:26). Christ personally predicts His second advent in words equally meaningful to all generations (Rev.22.12,20).

(vi) God's Kingdom. Though now only partially revealed, this kingdom is, nevertheless, "everlasting … from generation to generation" (Dan.4:3). However, it will fully appear when the final ten-nation power is crushed by the Stone, the returning Christ. Then "shall the God of heaven set up a kingdom" which will "stand for ever" (Dan.2:44).

Daniel stresses this aspect of an "everlasting kingdom" (Dan.4:34; 7:14,27). John also indicates the inauguration of the fullest expression of the kingdom, and also its duration - after the Tribulation he hears: "the kingdom of the world is become the kingdom of … Christ, and He shall reign for ever and ever" (Rev.11.15). The universality of Christ's kingdom is stressed by Daniel: "all the … nations … should serve Him" and "all dominions shall … obey Him" (Dan.7:14,27); a truth inherent in the title "KING OF KINGS AND LORD OF LORDS" (Rev.19:16). Daniel also points out that Old Testament saints will be given the kingdom (Dan.7:18,22), as will overcoming saints of this age (Rev.2:26; 3:21). They will all reign with Christ a thousand years before this old world is superseded by the eternal kingdom in the new earth (Rev.20:4; 21:1).

(vii) Angels and the Archangel. Daniel does not mention angels as such in his prophecies, though "His angel" is mentioned in relation to two events: the furnace and the lions' den (Dan.3:28; 6:22). In contrast, angels are mentioned seventy-five times in the Apocalypse, and in fact the entire Revelation was conveyed to John by an angel from the Lord (Rev.1:1; 22:6, 16). This topic has already been the subject of a previous paper. It is sufficient therefore to refer briefly to three matters. Firstly, Daniel wrote to God's earthly people concerning events on earth, whilst John wrote to His heavenly people to stress the primacy of the heavenly realm in shaping earth's destiny; hence his emphasis on angelic beings. Secondly, Daniel twice refers to Gabriel who appears as a man to instruct the seer (Dan.8:16; 9:21), whilst John makes no reference to him at all. Thirdly, Michael the archangel features in both books.

Daniel refers to him as "one of the chief princes" in his warrior-like capacity in conflict with apparent spiritual power behind the human ruler of Persia (Dan.10:13,20,21). He also indicates Michael's special responsibility as defender of God's earthly people, standing up prior to the "time of trouble" (Dan.12:7). John elaborates on this, depicting Michael at war with Satan in heaven, and the latter's ejection to earth, where he resumes his conflict, now against Michael's charge (Israel) thereby initiating the Tribulation (Rev.12.7-17).

7. Seers' Responses. The comparative study of the reactions of Daniel and John to divine revelation is very instructive. Much that Daniel saw and heard was frightening and grave. Consequently he says he was "grieved" and "troubled" (Dan.7:75). When he saw the "fierce" king who would arise he says, "I Daniel fainted, and was sick certain days; then I rose up and did the king's business" (Dan.8:27). Perhaps we shall only effectively conduct our King's business after first being distressed by a right view of the world's future. We are also challenged by Daniel's great intercessory prayer of confession after his discerning the imminence of the next event in God's programme. Chapter 9 warrants careful study. Although John sees more visions than Daniel—more terrible ones perhaps—generally he seems less disturbed than Daniel. However, there is a notable exception. Confronted by Christ among the lampstands, he says: "I fell at His feet as one dead" (Rev. 1:77). Also on two occasions he was so impressed by a heavenly messenger that he was about to worship him, before being suitably restrained (Rev.19:10; 22:8,9).

Three factors are suggested to explain why the seers' reactions are somewhat different.

Firstly, Daniel's visions were spread over many months, but John's presumably came in quick succession all on the Lord's day (Rev.1:10). John had little opportunity for interim reflection. Secondly, because John received the great revelations of God's ultimate universal victory, he was more likely to be elated than depressed. Thirdly, Daniel wrote when Gentile monarchs were being overthrown, and the Jewish nation was nearing the end of captivity—a time of heart-searching preparation for both groups. Daniel's distress, shared by his readers, would be the prelude to necessary repentance. In contrast, John received his revelations concerning Christian promises believed for a generation or more, when human history had still a long future unfolding ahead before those promises would finally materialise.

John's contemporaries, and saints for many centuries to follow, would need the strengthening assurance that God is in control—the joyful anticipation of His promises must be preserved. John's response sets the pattern, as seen below. Whilst Daniel ends on a note of assurance, "thou shalt rest, and shalt stand in thy lot, at the end of the days" (Dan.12:13), there is a ring of remoteness as to the time of this great blessing. On the other hand, John, captivated by the spirit of lively anticipation conveyed by his Lord's promise "I come quickly," replies in eager response, "Amen, come, Lord Jesus" (Rev.22:20).

Editors Comments

Comment A. Alternative interpretations of the vision of Daniel 7 have been widely debated. As to points raised in this article it may be noted— (i) that arguments based on verb tenses in prophecy are often of doubtful value e. g., Messiah's sufferings in Isaiah 53 are presented in the past tense. (ii) that the prolongation of the lives of three of the beasts may represent a continuing influence of certain powers through historical phases in which they have lost their once supreme position. (iii) that the suggestion of a major fulfilment in the end-time context would seem to be outweighed by symbolic detail which appears remarkably to identify past characteristics of the Babylonian, Medo-Persian, Greek and Roman Empires, e. g., —the winged lion, an apt symbol of the Babylonian empire; the bear raised up on one side, emphasizing Media's subservience to Persia; the agility and fierceness of the leopard, plus the impression of swiftness indicated by the wings, fittingly express the Grecian power under Alexander the Great, while the four heads point to the division of the empire among his generals; the ferocity and power of the fourth beast answer to the ruthless strength of the Roman empire.

Comment B. It would seem to be out of harmony with the overall prophetic picture to regard the ten toes as symbolic of the aggregate of world powers. For in each phase of Gentile dominion represented by the image of Daniel 2, a leading power rose to dominate the rest of the world. Similarly at the time of the end the Antichrist's power is seen to be based on a 10-kingdom confederacy, a "power block" which intimidates the world into submission (Rev.13:4).

Comment C. But was not Muslim domination during the "Church period" and therefore outside the ambit of Daniel's prophecy?

10

THE JUDGEMENT SEAT OF CHRIST AND THE GREAT WHITE THRONE—A COMPARATIVE STUDY (CLIVE BISHOP)

"It is appointed unto men once to die, and after this cometh judgement" (Heb.9:27). In these words Scripture unites all men, of all ages, in a common bond regardless of their attitude to God and His Son. Scripture further makes it clear that God is the Ruler of men, Lawgiver, and Judge (Jas.4:12). All men will face judge merit and two such judgements are referred to as the Judgement Seat of Christ and the Great White Throne. Both are comparable in that God is Judge (Heb.12:23) and that judgement is delivered through the person of Christ (2 Tim.4:8; Acts 10:42; Acts 17:31).

Men are judged "... by the man whom He hath ordained," but the unity of the Godhead in judgement is shown by the use of the terms "Judgement Seat of Christ" (2 Cor.5:10) and "Judgement Seat of God" (Rom.14:10) for the same event. The same principles of judgement apply to both; men are to be judged in accordance with the inherent justice of God (Rom.3:3,4) which is unassailable. In its execution the inviolate righteousness of God ensures that judgement will be utterly fair (Gen.18:25; Acts 17:31; Rom.3:6). The comparison extends also to the basis of judgement which rests on two main principles, namely a

47

man's works, and his attitude to God and to Christ. At both the Judgement Seat of Christ and at the Great White Throne it is works that are to be judged. Scripture speaks often of the "day of Judgement" and it is axiomatic that a man inevitably faces judgement, but faces it only once.

There is therefore an apparent paradox in the Lord's words "He that believeth on Him is not judged" (Jn 3:18) for no man can escape judgement. However, the word has the meaning of condemnation, and is virtually equivalent to the word 'krima', meaning a verdict or condemnation (Vine, 1940). The believer, by reason solely of faith in Christ, is assured that he need not appear before the Great White Throne; the verdict of that judgement was taken on his behalf by Christ, who is to be the instrument of judgement. But each will give to God an account of his life and be judged accordingly; for the believer this will be at the Judgement Seat of Christ. It is clear then that acceptance or rejection of Christ determines at which judgement seat those who live in the day of God's grace will appear. and equally no man will enter the eternal presence of God without the justification effected by the sacrifice of Christ.

This being so, both the Judgement Seat of Christ and the Great White Throne have to do with works (2 Cor.5:10; Rev.20:13). The difference is that no condemnation awaits those who appear before the Judgement Seat of Christ (Rom.8:1), whereas eternal destinies are weighed at the Great White Throne. Those at the Judgement Seat of Christ may suffer loss (1 Cor.3:13–15) but no more. The early chapters of the Roman letter give an insight into the way in which those at the Great White Throne will be judged. All kinds and conditions of men will appear and will be judged according to the light they had and to the revelation that was theirs (Rom.1:20). The judgement will be scrupulously fair; those who never knew the law will not be judged by it, but according to the law in their hearts and their conscience (Rom.2:12–16). It is perhaps appropriate to conclude with the comment that believers will also be judged according to light, for judgement begins at the House of God (Heb.10:30: 1 Pet.4:17).

11

THE RELATIONSHIP BETWEEN PAROUSIA, EPIPHANEIA AND APOKALUPSIS (ERIC ARCHIBALD)

Parousia

In the Revised Version text this Greek word is rendered in Matt.24:3 as 'coming,' where the marginal note gives the meaning 'presence.' The same Greek word is actually rendered as 'presence' in the R.V. text in 2 Corinthians 10:10; Philippians 1:26 and 2:12; but elsewhere, as in Matthew 24:3, the meaning given in the text is 'coming,' always accompanied by a reminder that the basic sense of the word 'parousia' is 'presence.' In ordinary Greek it could signify 'presence' or 'arrival', and was also the technical term for a royal visit. By derivation it implies 'being near' (Strong).

Epiphaneia

In 2 Thessalonians 2:8 the word 'epiphaneia' is translated in the R.V. as 'manifestation,' but elsewhere (1 Tim.6:14; 2 Tim.1: 10; 2 Tim.4:18; Tit.2:13) as 'appearing.' It can mean 'coming into view' or 'manfastation' in divine power.

Apokalupsis

In Romans 8:19 apokalupsis is translated 'revealing'. Elsewhere in the R.V. it is rendered by the word 'revelation.' The word can also mean 'unveiling' (Lk.2:32, R.V. margin).

In considering the relationship of these three words, it is important not to lose sight of the distinction between the coming of the Lord Jesus for the Church which is His Body, which is His coming to the air as Son of God (1 Thess.4:13-18; 1 Cor.15:23, 51), and on the other hand His coming to the earth as Son of Man with His saints and angels (2 Thess.2: 8). It is clear that the Lord Jesus will first come to the air, and at this glorious event both the living and the dead in Christ will be raised and brought into His presence. The word 'parousia' is used however in both 1 Cor.15:23 and 2 Thess.2:8. Josephus uses the word 'parousia' (Ant.3:80) with reference to the indwelling presence of God in the Temple.

In the New Testament, parousia is used of His earthly appearing (2 Tim.1:10), placed in the context of the purpose of God in grace. Apokalupsis is not used of the earthly life of the Lord, though indeed it was a revelation to the eye of faith (1 Cor.1:18). Epiphaneia expresses the brightness of the glory of the Lord's coming. It is especially relevant to His future coming to earth and His manifestation to the world. Only those who believed the truth saw the days of His flesh as the appearing of the Saviour Jesus Christ. For them there was also the knowledge of a day when His power would be outwardly evident and such as would welcome the revelation and coming of Antichrist would prove to have been deceived by a working of error. This assurance of the future appearing of the Anointed Christ would be a source of particular comfort to the saints to whom the Epistles were first written during the time of the Roman Empire.

In a past dispensation men of God believed in the overrule of God, and in divine intervention in world history, and they looked forward to the coming of the Messiah. The disciples were warned not to be misled regarding the time of His coming (parousia) as Son of Man (Matt.24:3). Aaron came back to the people of Israel with blessing (Lev.9:22). Christ, having been offered to bear the sins of many, shall appear a second time, apart from sin, to them that wait for Him unto salvation (Heb.9:28). At the coming (parousia) of the Son of God for believers of this dispensation (1 Thess.4: 5), faith will link up with sight and hope with realization, and we shall all be changed (1 Cor.15: 51).

Revelation (apokalupsis) is the disclosing of truth previously unknown, and in past ages God revealed Himself by signs and intimations, by the oracle of the Urim and Thummim, and by His holy prophets. He made Himself known as Creator and the Living God, and revealed His counsel as governing the course of history, requiring holiness and obedience from His people. It was not man by reason unveiling God, but the Spirit bringing conviction of the truth of God, privilege being matched by responsibility. In Romans 4:23 the dealings of God with Abraham are shown to have a present application, but central to the revelation of God is the Son of God who reveals the Father (Matt.11:27). It is through the Spirit that God revealed the word of the Cross (1 Cor.2:10), the revelation of Jesus Christ (Gal.1:12).

The scope of this revelation is immense, having expression in the future as in 1 Corinthians 1:7, 'waiting for the revelation of Jesus Christ; who shall also confirm you to the end, that ye be unreproveable in the day of our Lord Jesus Christ', and again in 2 Thessalonians 1:7, "and to you that are afflicted, rest with us at the revelation of the Lord Jesus from heaven with the angels of His power." In the book of Revelation, the revelation of Jesus Christ prepares the saints for tribulation by revealing heavenly and eternal things and the destiny of the world to be bound up with Jesus Christ. Revelations of the Lord were made known to the apostle Paul (2 Corinthians 12:1). Paul desired that the Ephesians should be granted a spirit of wisdom and revelation in the knowledge of the Lord Jesus Christ (Eph.1:17; comp. Phil.3:15). The lesson for us in these three words is "The Lord is at hand" (Phil.4:5).

12

REIGNING WITH CHRIST - A STUDY OF DELEGATED AUTHORITY (ANDY MCILREE)

Within the great eternal purpose of God the millennial day will be ushered in, bearing the same assurance as the day through which the land shall be cleansed: "Behold, it cometh, and it shall be done" (Ezek.39:8). Throughout the tribulation period angels will be instrumental in proclaiming the wrath of God, "having great authority" (Rev.18:1). Yet they little compare with the One who will come forth for Armageddon and for the judgement of the living nations having "all authority", thus making the scene ready for 1,000 years of order and unparalleled peace. For such a programme it is first decreed, as if by way of an early delegation of authority, that there should be the binding, casting, shutting and sealing of Satan at the hand of an angel (Rev.20:1-3). All manner of deception will be dispelled and the day and the servant will take character from the One whose Kingdom it is. Every trace of earthly administration with its puny earthly personnel will be removed to make way for the perfection of theocratic government. Then the truly Righteous. One (Ps.1), the rightful King (Ps.2), will take up His reign, for "the kingdom of the world is become the kingdom of our Lord, and of His Christ ..."

Of this time, Scripture is expressive as to the character of His reign. In Rev.12:5 we read

" ... who is to rule all the nations with a rod of iron." The word "rule" (Gk. poimaino) indicates that whilst operating firmly as ruler He will do so as a shepherd. This firmness is in harmony with gentleness as seen in Is.40:10,11—"His arm shall rule for Him ..." ; and yet "He shall feed His flock like a shepherd, He shall gather the lambs in His arm, and carry them in His bosom, and shall gently lead those that give suck." Both psalmist and angel present the One who will reign (Ps.93:1; Lk.1:33). The Lamb (Gk. amnos) who came as sacrifice will then come, still as the Lamb (Gk. arnion), but apparelled with majesty. At last, earth will know a time of certain rule for "He shall judge the world with righteousness, and the peoples with His truth" (Ps.96:13). Only then will be revealed the fulfilment of prophecy and prayer as foreshown by Hos.2:21 — "... the heavens ... shall answer the earth," and by the Lord Himself—"Thy will be done on earth, as it is in heaven." Through the same prophet the word had been given that "Israel shall abide many days without king ... prince, ... sacrifice, ... ephod ..." (3:4).

In the millennial day, with these relationships restored, every man will be able to "sit under his vine and under his fig tree," illustrated in Solomon's day when "all the princes ... gave the hand under Solomon" (1 Chr.29:24 RVM). Of the Lord, Zechariah has written, "He ... shall sit and rule upon His throne; and He shall be a priest upon His throne" (Zech.6:13). So then, He who will return to take up His reign as King is also the promised Priest, appearing "a second time, apart from sin, to them that wait for Him, unto salvation" (Heb.9:28). As King-Priest, His delegation of authority will therefore be twofold, embracing those who will serve outwardly, as the exponents of His infallible judgements, together with those who in priestly capacity will serve inwardly in the charge of the sanctuary.

David as King

Under the King-Priest, David will serve as the servant-king (Ezek.37:24). He is marked out by God as "My servant" but Israel's king, in fulfilment of the covenant given through Nathan in 2 Samuel 7, relating to "... thine house ... thy kingdom ... thy throne" (v.16). No doubt David wakened out of sleep to learn the content of the covenant, yet having served the counsel of God, "he fell on sleep" (Acts 13:36), out of which he shall again wake to engage in its service. In that day the former servant (Heb. ebed, often signifying slave) will be prince (Heb. exalted). The character of his service is clearly seen in his being "over" as king and as shepherd (Heb. roeho). Twice God says "and he shall feed (Heb. raah) them" (Ezek.34:23), which is significantly linked with his rule (v.24) (Heb. nasi-prince, ruler).

The Twelve Apostles

"Ye shall sit on thrones judging the twelve tribes of Israel" (Lk.22:30). To those who had shared His rejection, and had continued with Him in His temptations (Lk.22:28), the Lord gave the assurance of sharing with Him "when the Son of Man shall sit on the throne of His glory" (Matt.19:28); a fitting reward to the faithful servants who had followed Him and heard the promise in reply to Peter's question, "Lo, we have left all and followed Thee: what then shall we have"? (Matt.19:27).

It is interesting to note in John 21:15-17, the Lord's words to Peter "feed (Gr. bosko) ... tend (Gr. poimdno) ... feed (bosko)," thus showing again, as with David, the importance of feeding in relation to ruling. In the days of His flesh they continued (Gr. didmend—to remain throughout) daily with Him, and having been marked out as His, they were also prepared to suffer (Acts 5:41).

Saints of this Dispensation

"Know ye not that the saints shall judge the world?" (1 Cor.6:2). Whilst the apostles are in the forefront because of their singular association with the Lord, it is evident that the characteristics found in them must also be seen in those from this dispensation. One likeness is seen in Rev.2:26,27 — "he that overcometh, and he that keepeth my works unto the end, to him will I give authority over the nations: and he shall rule them with a rod of iron." A second condition is seen in 2 Tim.2:12: "if we endure (Greek. hupomeno. A.V. suffer), we shall also reign." Being therefore governed by such conditions, those selected will be given positions of authority which also will know gradation as expressed in the parable of the pounds in Luke 19.

Saints of the Great Tribulation

The Lord Himself spoke of this time as "such as hath not been from the beginning of the world until now, no, nor ever shall be." In this, the fiercest time of conflict, there will still be those who will remain true to the testimony of Jesus—unto the end—even if termination is through suffering and death (Rev.20:4). These will have held positively their faithfulness "for the testimony" and "for the word" whilst rejecting the call to false worship and satanic associations. With all brought together, marshalled by earth's rightful Sovereign, God will bring about His purpose so that "judgement was given to the saints of the Most High; and the time came that the saints possessed the kingdom" (Dan.7:22).

In a world that will know changes affecting topography, elements, and animals, men will see the greatest change in the formation and outworking of this great administration of which Isaiah wrote, — "Behold, a King shall reign in righteousness, and princes shall rule in judgement" (32:1). Working out from Jerusalem these princes will operate in their delegated sphere, maintaining the standards of righteous rule, exercising it daily in the midst of successive generations so that "in His days shall the righteous flourish; and abundance of peace" (Ps.72:7).

The Sons of Zadok (Heb. Righteous).

Finally we come to the important area of priestly activity as outlined in Ezekiel 44. To them will be given the charge of the sanctuary in appreciation of having kept the charge of a former day, in all faithfulness. They will be engaged in the offering of restored animal sacrifices—"offerings in righteousness"—offering the fat (Heb. the best) and the blood (v.15) and in the presence of the Lord they will fully see what was foreshown in those of the earlier dispensation. They also will have regulations to fulfil affecting their garments (v.17), their hair (v.20) and their marriage (v.22) etc. So then, in each setting we see something of the great reign of the King-priest of whom it is written: "He shall come down like rain upon the mown grass: as showers that water the earth" (Ps.72:6). In such a perfect setting He "shall reign in mount Zion ... and before His ancients gloriously" (Is.24:23).

13

THE ORDER OF RESURRECTION (IAN PENN)

"Jesus saith unto her, Thy brother shall rise again. Martha saith unto Him, I know that he shall rise again in the resurrection at the last day. Jesus said unto her, I am the resurrection, and the life: he that believeth on Me, though he die, yet shall he live" (Jn 11: 23-25).

The welcoming of the Lord Jesus into the Bethany household ensured His entrance and we may confidently surmise that it was therefore one of the most instructed of its day. Martha's reply may then be taken as representative of what was understood of resurrection until the coming of the Lord Jesus. She linked the resurrection of her departed brother with a definite point in time. And it is the measure of her despair not only that this was the last event in time but also, it may be implied, that it must await a time when all, irrespective of their dealings with God, will be raised. But the Lord Jesus spoke Lazarus up from the dead and out of the tomb in a token of what He was to accomplish for his race. At the hour of universal resurrection He will again speak up the dead and bring their bodies out of their graves, for He said "the hour cometh, in which all that are in the tombs shall hear His voice, and shall come forth; they that have done good, unto the resurrection of life; and they that have done ill, unto the resurrection of judgement" (John 5:28,29).

Whence, because of its subordination to Christ, its universal application, its occurrence at the end of time as we know it, and the entrance into life or death (the second death) of those who are raised, it is clear that this is the resurrection spoken of in association with the Great White Throne (Rev.20:11). But the final paragraph of Revelation 20 is so connected with the preceding three that an unbroken sequence in time is described. In this an earlier, first resurrection precedes the final resurrection by the period of one thousand years mentioned throughout the chapter. No resurrection intervenes (Revelation 20:5) and therefore the final resurrection is implicitly the second resurrection. All who are raised in the first resurrection are believers for over them (unlike certain raised in the final resurrection) the second death has no power. One group of believers is especially mentioned consisting of "them that had been beheaded for the testimony of Jesus, and for the word of God, and such as worshipped not the beast, neither his image, and received not the mark upon their forehead and upon their hand."

This group is easily identified as comprising those who died for Him during the immediately preceding period of great tribulation, when God punishes men who are alive on the earth and who terrorise each other, and which is terminated by the coming of the Lord Jesus to the earth to reign (Matt.24:15-31; Rev.13:7-18). But there are others in this first resurrection for, following the coming of the wrath of God is "the time of the dead to be judged, and the time to give their reward to Thy servants the prophets, and to the saints, and to them that fear Thy name, the small and the great" (Rev.11:18), and the time when "many of them that sleep in the dust of the earth shall awake, some to everlasting life" (Dan.12:2). The first resurrection, which is restricted to believers, includes such as Daniel, who shall stand in his lot at the end of the great tribulation (Dan.12:12-13); Abraham, Isaac and Jacob (Matt.8:11; Lk.13:28); David (Ezek.37:25) who shall enjoy the ensuing kingdom; and a whole host of lesser renown many of whom will have responded to the preaching e. g. of a prophet like Zechariah who, when the people of God were at a low ebb, revived them with the promise of experiencing just such a national greatness beyond anything they had known.

The first resurrection does not include believers of the present day of grace because "the Lord Himself shall descend from heaven, with a shout, with the voice of the archangel, and with the trump of God: and the dead in Christ shall rise first: then we that are alive, that are left, shall together with them be caught up in the clouds, to meet the Lord in the air" (1 Thess.4:16,17), and the whole point of the succeeding verses is that participants in this resurrection, who are all in Christ, will not pass through the day of wrath and great tribulation. This resurrection therefore precedes the first resurrection (in fact by the period of at least seven years). Time and season are not associated with this resurrection which takes place at the coming of the Lord to the air for the Church which is His Body; an event which has always been regarded by those in Christ as imminent (John 14:3: Heb.10:37; Rev.22:20). Indeed so much so that some wrongly taught in Thessalonica that this resurrection had passed and that they were living in the day of wrath! (2 Thess.2:2).

In summary then, 1 Thess.4:75 and Revelation 20 establish a definite sequence of moments of resurrection and expand the statement: "each in his own order: Christ the firstfruits; then they that are Christ's, at His coming. Then cometh the end" (1 Corinthians 15:23- 24). At the end of this dispensation is the resurrection of its saints who are in Christ. At the end of the ensuing period, some seven or more years later, is the first resurrection in which believers of past ages (Rev.11:18) as well as the martyrs of the immediately preceding tribulation will be raised. Finally at the end of the thousand years the rest of the dead will be raised. Each moment of resurrection is associated with the Lord Jesus Christ who will come to the air with archangel voice for His Church; to the earth when other saints will be raised and when He will reign: and who speaks the rest of the dead out of Hades and their graves at the last day.

Each group of resurrected ones is then judged by Him. They that are Christ's receive rewards following each of the two earlier moments of resurrection, while the rest of the dead are judged at the Great White Throne at the last day, when those whose names are not written in the Lamb's book of life pass into the shame and everlasting contempt of which Daniel spoke concerning his people in that clause which is parenthetical both in content as well as time of fulfilment (Dan.12:2). The resurrection of the Lord Jesus Christ thus marks a distinct turning point in the history of mankind. Whereas before, the various great periods in which God had dealt with men may be viewed as ending with human failure and consequent judgements, afterwards they are marked by resurrection particularly of believers who have died in the immediately preceding period. (As a token of these sure things we may cite the apparently localised raising of saints in Jerusalem at the time of the Lord's resurrection (Matt.27:55) and in the future (Rev.11.11)). Sleep till the last day is not for them; instead, a foretaste of eternity, a fulness of salvation which daily becomes nearer than when they first believed.

As it is written, "For if, by the trespass of the one, death reigned through the one; much more shall they that receive the abundance of grace and of the gift of righteousness reign in life through the one, even Jesus Christ" (Rom.5:17).

14

THE DAY OF CHRIST AND THE DAY OF THE LORD (COLIN BROOKS)

It must be evident to the most casual reader of the Scriptures that God's purposes so far as His dealings with men are concerned are seen to be related to very clearly defined eras. The references to "the time of the promise" (Acts 7: 17) and "the fulness of the time" (Gal.4:4), support this view. Both marked a very important stage in the fulfilment of God's purposes. There seems no doubt that in the understanding of the apostles the incarnation of the Lord Jesus marked the end of one such era and the commencement of another. Indeed, Hebrews 1:2 speaks of the "end of these days", and Hebrew 9:26 of "the end of the ages". In 1 Corinthians 10:11 Paul addresses the believers of his day and says: "upon whom the ends of the ages are come."

Over against this we have the word of Peter in Acts 2: 17 on the day of Pentecost quoting from the prophecy of Joel and applying the words "the last days" to the time at which he spoke. [Peter did apply this to the pouring out of the Spirit at Pentecost, but the fulfilment of the prophecy is still in the future—Eds.]. The apostle John also in 1 John 2:18 speaks of "the last hour", and the Lord Himself in John 6:39, 40 and John 12:48 spoke of the "last day." These scriptures, together with many more, would indicate that this time referred to as the last day or days embraces not just a specific event, but actually spans

61

a considerable length of time. The resurrection of John 6 and the judgement of John 12 belong to two different occasions. Although others would take a different view, we conclude, therefore, that the last days commence with the birth of the Lord and carry us forward to the final climax of God's dealings with this present earth.

If this be so, we must therefore look for the other important events spoken of in the Scriptures as taking place somewhere between these two points in time. Without doubt the one of paramount importance to the believer is the rapture of the Church which is His Body, something unique and peculiar to this dispensation of grace. 'Rapture' as such is not a New Testament expression but is the event described by Paul in 1 Thessalonians 4:17 as a 'catching up'. It is this same event which Paul has in view when he speaks of: — the day of Jesus Christ—Phil.1:6 the day of Christ—Phil. 1:10 the day of Christ—Phil.2:16 the day of our Lord Jesus Christ—1 Cor.1:8 the day of our Lord Jesus—2 Cor.1:14 the revelation of our Lord Jesus Christ—1 Cor.1:7. It will be noticed that in almost all these scriptures what Paul has in view is not only the appearing of the Lord Jesus, but also the believer's presenting himself before the Lord for His appraisal and scrutiny.

Paul speaks even more specifically of this aspect in 2 Corinthians 5:10 as the 'Judgement Seat of Christ.' These two events would seem to be almost synchronous in the apostle's teaching. It is interesting to note that in all the above scriptures where he refers to the believer's assessment before the Lord nowhere does he speak of "the day of the Lord." We judge therefore that this is something quite separate and distinct from the above. However, before passing on to this, perhaps we would do well to ponder the implications the "day of Christ" will have for each of us. It will bring to every believer what Peter describes as "the end of our faith," "an inheritance incorruptible" and "the grace to be brought unto us." What a prospect to cheer and encourage each heart, what an incentive to seek to implement the exhortation by John: "He that hath this hope set on him purifieth himself ... (1 Jn 3:3)!

There is, however, the other solemn aspect of that day, and of course this is the moment of truth for each one of us as "each one is made manifest" (visible) before the Lord. Paul uses some very strong language, and in 1 Corinthians 3:10-15 borrows a telling analogy from the testing of the fire. He speaks of work good and bad. Of reward and loss. Of our works surviving the fire and the possibility of their being burned. Finally, he speaks of the possibility of the believer himself being saved "so as through fire." As we ponder these solemn possibilities again we may recall the lines: — In view of that devouring flame, Be this our prayer and this our aim, In Him may we abide. To think only of that day as one for receiving of rewards does less than justice to the clear statements of scripture. Paul put it another way when he said: "work out your own salvation with fear and trembling" (Phil.2:12).

Unlike the "day of Christ," the "day of the Lord" has its roots in the Old Testament prophecies, especially those of Bible Studies Joel (2:1,31; 3:14) and Jeremiah (30:7,8). Peter, on the day of Pentecost, cited Joel (Acts 2:20). Here this day is associated with the judgement of God first of all on His sinful and backsliding people but also on the nations round about (Joel 13: 12). It would be perhaps wrong to conclude that this judgement is an end in itself but rather it is seen as not only the retribution of God on sin but also as a process of chastening and purifying and refining with a view to ensuing blessing. This is supported by New Testament references to the same day. The Lord refers to this (Matt.24:16,21,29) and Paul also (2 Thess.2:2). We know, too, from the book of Revelation that not only Israel but the nations also are to experience those dreadful days when the judgements of God will be unleashed on a godless age. For Israel this is the "time of Jacob's trouble" (Jer.30:7) and for the nations a day of "flaming fire and a day of vengeance" (2 Thess.1:8).

Fearful as these days will be, so fearful that "were they not shortened, no flesh would be saved", yet nevertheless they will herald the dawning of the glorious Millennium, a time of unprecedented blessing so far as this earth is concerned. Isaiah, Ezekiel, Zechariah and others speak of these coming days of divine healing and blessing on this earth. A day when above all "a king shall reign in righteousness." As we return to the Epistle to the Thessalonians we are reminded that we are not sons of the night or darkness but rather "sons of the day." Paul also states (1 Thess.5:9) that "God appointed us not unto wrath," and again "Even Jesus, which delivereth us from the wrath to come" (1 Thess.1:10), clear evidence to some that the Church the Body will not be present in those dark days which we have been considering, but will have been "caught up" to meet the Lord in the air. With such a hope we would emulate the Thessalonians and "wait for His Son from heaven."

15

WHAT IS 'THE LORD'S DAY'? (GEORGE KENNEDY)

In two places in the Holy Scriptures there is a Greek word, an adjective, 'kuriakos', derived from 'kurios', meaning 'lord'. The two places are 1 Corinthians 11:20 (the Lord's supper) and Revelation 1:10, where it refers to the first day of the week (as is hereafter shown), and it is to be distinguished from the genitive or possessive kuriou (meaning 'of lord') which occurs in many other places, such as 2 Thessalonians 2:2. The meaning of kuriakos is "of or for a lord or master." However, since kuriakos is an adjective, there is no exact English equivalent which can be used to translate it, although 'lordly' is sometimes used. The words 'imperial' and 'dominical' have also been used.

The "Lord's Day" of Revelation 1:10 is not the same as the "Day of the Lord" which is a period of time over 1,000 years long, beginning at the end of the Great Tribulation and finishing with the passing away of the heaven and earth before the Great White Throne Judgement (Acts 2:20; 1 Thess.5:2-3; 2 Thess.2:2; 2 Pet.3:10). If the apostle John had been in the Spirit (Rev.1:10) on the day of the Lord, then most of the Revelation would not have been written because most of the contents of the Revelation have occurred or will occur before that Day begins. The apostle John was in a certain place (the island of Patmos - Rev.1:9) on a certain day (the Lord's or Lordly day - verse 10). The

65

question then remains whether this Lord's Day is the weekly sabbath day or the first day of the week, Saturday or Sunday.

There are a number of references to the first day of the week as the Lord's Day in very early writings, dating from about 100 A.D., that is very shortly after the book of the Revelation was written, which most commentators place at about 95 A.D. Ignatius (martyred 115 A.D.) makes a difference between the sabbath and the Lord's Day and affirms that the latter is the resurrection day. The "Epistle of Barnabus" (about 120 A.D.) indicates the general practice of early Christians in regard to the "eighth day", which is the first day of the week. The "Didache" or "Teaching of the Apostles" (120 A.D. or earlier) says, "On the Lord's own day gather yourselves together and break bread and give thanks." Justin Martyr, Ireneus and Tertullian (140-200 A.D.) refer to Sunday, the first day of the week, being the Lord's Day. No evidence whatsoever exists that Christians in the early centuries regarded the sabbath as the Lord's day or that they ever kept the Lord's supper on the sabbath day.

Having now noted that the Lord's day is not the same as the Day of the Lord and having heard the testimony of the early fathers (so-called) that the Lord's day was the resurrection day, we will now consider the keeping of the sabbath. Whether or not it is the Christian's present duty to keep and observe the sabbath day has been a problem for some children of God. They read the ten commandments and ask if it is not right that the other nine should be obeyed and if so then why not that commandment which says, "remember the sabbath day." In this article we look at the question of sabbath day observance, and firstly we answer the question with which we have begun. The other nine commandments are all repeated in the New Testament as part of the present will of God. On the other hand there is no reference whatever by example or instruction to a Christian observance of the sabbath (seventh day).

It will help us to understand the place of the sabbath day if we look at the Biblical references to it and note also where the Bible does not refer to it. The first reference to the sabbath day (sabbath means rest) is in Genesis 2:2-3 where God rested because His work was finished and it was very good in His sight. (But note that it was not called the sabbath day). That rest was for God and it followed a finished work which had been according to the will and word of God. Adam had no part in the doing of that work - it had been God's work - and Adam was brought into the enjoyment of it. Adam's first full day on earth was the day of God's rest in which Adam was given the wonderful privilege of enjoying the work of God in all its completeness: "the works were finished from the foundation of the world" (Heb.4:3).

Adam was not commanded to rest every seventh day. God put him into the Garden of Eden to dress it and to keep it and He gave no commandment to Adam to observe a sabbath day. The only commandment was that he should not eat of the tree of the knowledge of good and evil. Every day was Adam's responsibility to dress and to keep the Garden. Adam in his innocence did not observe the sabbath day because he was in the full enjoyment of God's finished work.

After the Fall Adam was put out of the Garden of Eden. God gave him no commandment to keep the sabbath day but rather said to him: "Cursed is the ground for thy sake; in toil shalt thou eat of it all the days of thy life" (Gen.3:17). Sin brought a curse and with that curse came toil and there was no rest, no sabbath. For 2,500 years from the time of the Garden of Eden there was no commandment and no provision concerning the sabbath day. Noah is not commended because he kept the sabbath nor was the world condemned in the Flood because they kept it not. Noah, Abraham, Isaac and Jacob in their covenants with God had no obligation to keep the sabbath. Job, who may have lived during the time of the Egyptian bondage, seems to have known nothing of the sabbath although we are told much of his righteousness and good works.

It was not until a people was redeemed out of slavery and had been baptized in the Red Sea that God took up the sabbath day with man. It is clear from Nehemiah 9:13-14 that God had not previously ordained sabbath keeping for man until Mount Sinai; "Thou ... madest known unto them Thy holy sabbath."

Because God made it known, it is clear that it was not previously made known. And then it was not until He made provision for them in the manna (Ex.16:22-30). The children of Israel fed upon the divinely provided food; they rested in a provision which God gave them out of heaven (Neh.9:15; Jn 6:31), so that it was made miraculously possible that they rested on the sabbath.

The Lord gave Israel the ten commandments, His holy law that was the covenant between Himself and them wherein He would be their God and they would be His people, the kingdom of God. Notice what the fourth commandment says: "Remember the sabbath day to keep it holy. Six days shalt thou labour and do all thy work: but the seventh day is a sabbath unto the Lord thy God: in it thou shalt not do any work" (Ex.20:8-10). The sabbath day was relative to labour and work. The Law is all of works. The sabbath day existed because of man's work. He had to cease from work and rest unto God. The Israelite did not begin his week with rest. He worked and the prospect of rest was at the end. He looked forward to rest and not backward to it. If we understand the place of the Law (it is our tutor, guide or conductor to bring us to Christ) and if we learn its lesson we will see the significance of the sabbath. Before the cross of Christ, men of faith looked forward to what was to come. The Christian today is not looking forward to when work will be finished but is resting on a finished work. Like Adam, who began his existence in the divine rest, the Christian today is resting in the finished work of Christ who said upon the cross: "It is finished."

In Exodus 31:12-17 God clearly defined the extent of sabbath day observance. Moses was commanded to speak to the children of Israel. It was a sign between God and them. "Wherefore the children of Israel shall keep the sabbath ... a sign between Me and the children of Israel." God said to the Israelites "thou wast a servant in the land of Egypt ... therefore the Lord thy God commanded thee to keep the sabbath day" (Deut.5:15). The sabbath belongs to that covenant made with Israel and has to do with their national identity as God's people whether in the past or future (e.g. Matt.24:20, Is.66:23, Ezek.46:1). During this present day of grace Israel is set aside nationally.

The sabbath day was a vital and integral part of the Law which was a shadow of the things to come (see Heb.10:1). On that day the shewbread was set in order in the Tabernacle (Lev.24:8 and note the end of the verse; would any make this applicable to Christians today?); extra lambs were slain on the sabbath day (Num.28:9,10). Under the terms of the sabbath day the Israelites could gather no sticks, light no fires, carry no burden, do no work, sell nothing and buy nothing. They were restricted in the distance of travel. I remember having a meal on a Saturday in a hospital canteen where a charge was made for the food. I offered to pay but my money was refused and yet the price was entered in a book so that I could pay later. That is legalism. The technicality of not taking the money did not mean that a sale had not been made. If the sabbath is still in force so are all its obligations. The sabbath was for a people which existed nationally separated from the Gentiles, not only religiously but in commerce and all else.

The sabbath and its obligations continued until the resurrection of Christ. From that time it is the first day of the week that predominates in the disciple experience. The first day of the week is not a sabbath. The sabbath precept was part of the Law. The Lord observed the sabbath, not as part of the New Covenant but of the Old. "God sent forth His Son ... born under the Law" (Gal.4:4) and having kept the Law perfectly He is now the end of the Law unto righteousness to every one that believes (Rom.10:4).

Sometimes it is argued that the apostles observed the sabbath because they preached to the Jews on the sabbath (Acts 13:14,44; 17:2 etc.). It might just as readily be argued that they believed the temple to be God's house because they met there to preach (Acts 2:46; 3:1; 5:20). The fact is that they went to the places where the people were on the days that the people gathered. These were not the church gatherings of the Christians but the times when the apostles had a "word of exhortation for the people" (Acts 13:15). The church activities of disciples in fellowship together were more particularly marked out as being on the first day of the week (Acts 20:7; 1 Cor.16:2).

16

WITNESSES IN REVELATION AND SCRIPTURE (ROBERT SHAW)

A witness is "one who testifies to that which he has seen or heard or understands" and the keynote is to be found in the dual reference to Christ in the book of Revelation, "The faithful and true Witness" (Rev.1:5, 3:14). In fact, the word "martyr" in the English language, a transliteration of the Greek word 'martus', possibly signifies the ultimate in faithful witnessing. The effect of witnessing is twofold. Firstly, testimony may be borne to a person, event, truth or other matter. Secondly, it may explain or clarify an issue or otherwise shed light upon the darkness. The use of the word "witness" is extensive in the Old Testament concerning those inanimate things which testified to the making of agreements or covenants: e. g. the pillar and heap of stones relating to Laban's covenant with Jacob at Gilead (Gen.31:44-52).

The deeper significance is that God witnessed the covenant which had been made. God, in turn, used as His witness the faithful and true word in song and precept, which He skilfully placed in the mouths and upon the hearts of the sons of Israel before entering Canaan, testimony within to act as chastisement from a righteous God in evil days and, perchance, to bring them to repentance (Deut.31:21,26). In addition, God shows Himself (witnesses) to men through His servants. The Lord said, "He that hath seen Me hath seen the Father"

71

John 14:9; Heb.1:1, 2). The need for a witness is often determined by the condition of the people to whom he is sent. God chose Noah and, the condition of the people being one of extreme ungodliness, Noah became a "preacher of righteousness." His witness condemned the world. He was a man who enjoyed communion with God; therefore God entrusted His message to him. Godly men and women, though few in number, interspersed among their fellows, can have a marked effect, the extent of which is known to God alone (Matt.5:13-16). In the day of destruction of ungodly men, yet future, the testimony of the lives of godly men will play no small part. So whether by object, word or servant, "He left not Himself without witness" (Acts 14:17).

The Laodicean church in the book of Revelation was far removed in condition from the mind of the Lord. They had a false picture of themselves; they treasured false values and consequently were at the threshold of spiritual bankruptcy. Over against these, however, is "the Amen, the faithful and true Witness", in absolute harmony with the mind of God. He sets His riches out and counsels them to buy, that they may become rich, that they may clothe themselves, and that they may see that communion may be restored and that they may enter into fullest fellowship with Christ as overcomers.

In Revelation 11:1-13 we read of certain events in Jerusalem surrounding two witnesses who, we judge, will prophesy in the first half of Daniel's seventieth week. Although events parallel to those miraculous powers given to the two witnesses are recorded during the lives of Moses and Elijah, we cannot allow speculation to determine their identity. The words, "I will give unto my two witnesses," explain the origin of the powers vested in them (verses 5,6) and of the message which they will speak. God will fit them for the preaching of a call to repentance, manifested in the reference to garments of mourning (sackcloth), yet it would appear that those mighty deeds and truthful words which will torment men will merely have the effect of slowing down the sinful pursuits of those that dwell on the earth in that day, "a day of pride, fulness of bread and prosperous ease."

The witnesses are described as the two olive trees (the tree of oil for testimony) and the two lampstands (that which illumines) and these two features are prime essentials, as has already been stated, to the function of witnessing. They are God's faithful prophets, "standing before the Lord," and in their faithfulness they will experience the ultimate of martyrdom. But after three days and a half, corresponding to the years of their witness, they will be raised and will ascend publicly into heaven in the cloud.

In Revelation 7:1-10 we are introduced to a band of witnesses with a world-wide message. These are the 144,000 sealed witnesses from every tribe of the children of Israel (except Dan) and they will testify in Antichrist's kingdom concerning the forthcoming millennial reign of Christ. They will have great success by the help of the Spirit (Joel 2:28-32), akin to that of the early days of apostolic ministry, for the time is short. The result cannot be measured (Rev.7:9) and the reward is great (Matt.25:31-46). As we review the faithfulness and dedication of witnesses gone before and yet to come, the clear lessons must not be lost to those whom He has called to witness for Him in the day of grace.

17

ANGELS IN REVELATION AND SCRIPTURE (W. BUNTING)

It is interesting to note that in the book of the Revelation angels are referred to some 68 times. They are mentioned in 19 of the 22 chapters. We are told in the first verse that the Revelation was sent and signified (or communicated) by His angel unto His servant John, whereas twice in the last chapter, in verses 6 and 16 we have confirmation of the part played by an angel in communicating this remarkable book. In the Old Testament angels are mentioned 109 times, and 172 times in the New Testament. Contrary to the popular view, the word in its Greek form 'angelos' (angel or messenger) is a masculine noun. As far as the present writer is aware, there is no instance in the Scriptures of the manifestation of an angel in female form.

The Nature of Angels

What do we mean by nature? The Oxford dictionary defines the word as "essential qualities." In the Authorized Version of Hebrews 2:16, where reference is made to the incarnation of Christ, the words "the nature of" are in italics, and do not form part of the original. These words are inserted to assist the English reader. The Revised Version reads: "For verily not of angels doth He take hold, but He taketh hold of the seed of Abraham." In order that

Christ should effect salvation through death, it was necessary that He should be a sharer in blood and flesh, and in His great stoop He passed angels by.[1]

We may infer from this that angels do not share blood and flesh, and that they are not subject to death. This latter statement seems to command special note. When the Lord answered the Sadducees regarding those worthy to attain to the resurrection we find these words in Luke 20:36: "Neither can they die any more: for they are equal unto the angels; and are sons of God, being sons of the resurrection." The citation in Hebrews 2:6-8 is from Psalm 8. It is understood that "man" referred to in this Psalm is "frail mortal man," and he is of an order lower than that of angels. While Christ, to achieve salvation, was for a little while lower than the angels, He was even then crowned with glory and honour, that by the grace of God He should taste death for every man. When John, who heard and saw the wonderful things recorded in the Revelation, was later constrained to fall down and worship at the feet of the angel, he was restrained by the angel who said, "See thou do it not: I am a fellow-servant with thee and with thy brethren the prophets, and with them which keep the words of this book: worship God" (Rev.22:9).

That there are different grades or orders of angels, performing different functions, seems to be borne out in the references to Michael and Gabriel. The former is named as "one of the chief princes" (Dan.10:13) and as "the archangel" in Jude 9. Michael's activities lie in the field of helping those attacked by Satan, and he will lead the war in heaven described in Revelation 12:7-12. On the other hand Gabriel, who stands in the presence of God, seems to be the revealer or instructor. When Daniel saw the vision and sought to

---

[1] Alternative note on Hebrews 2:16 - To 'take hold' is from epilambano and is used in the sense of coming to one's help (compare Matt.14:31 and Mk.8:23). Angels did not need to be delivered from the fear of death. The seed of Abraham does. The Lord became incarnate to bring help to men. It is suggested that the seed of Abraham would include all believers of both old and new dispensations—the children of faith. The American Revised renders it 'He giveth help to the seed of Abraham.' In the sense in which the phrase is used here, we judge it excludes the Galatians 3:16 reference—James Martin

understand it, he heard the command: "Gabriel, make this man to understand the vision" (Dan.8:16). Later when Daniel was praying, Gabriel drew near and instructed him, and made Daniel skilful of understanding. As the revealer, Gabriel appeared to Zacharias (Lk.1:19) and to Mary (Lk.1:26).

The Work of Angels

In considering this aspect we are helped by the writer of the letter to the Hebrews who, when referring to angels states, "Are they not all ministering spirits, sent forth to do service for the sake of them that shall inherit salvation?" (Heb.1:14). The thought is of rendering aid or service, and it is well to note that it is on behalf of them that shall inherit salvation. The work of angels was fully appreciated by David— "Bless the LORD, ye angels of His: Ye mighty in strength, that fulfill His word, Hearkening unto the voice of His word. Bless the Lord, all ye His hosts; ye ministers of His, that do His pleasure" (Ps.103:20,21). Following a period of deep distress and subsequent deliverance, David wrote one of the choicest words found in his many psalms: "The angel of the LORD encampeth round about them that fear Him, And delivereth them" (Ps.34:7). In this connection we may learn from the experience of Elisha and his servant at Dothan. They were encircled by enemies, and in desperation the servant said, "Alas, my master! how shall we do?"

It was then that Elisha prayed, "LORD, I pray Thee, open his eyes, that he may see. And the LORD opened the eyes of the young man; and he saw: and, behold, the mountain was full of horses and chariots of fire round about Elisha" (2 Kin.6:17). A few examples follow of the appearance of angels to help men and women in need of succour. To Gideon (Judg.6:11), Manoah's wife (Judg.13:5), Daniel (Dan.6:22), Peter (Acts 12:7), Paul (Acts 27:23). The statement in Matt.18:10 regarding angels and children is worthy of special note. Angels and Christ. Prior to the birth of Christ the angel Gabriel appeared to Mary and conveyed the profound news, "The Holy Spirit shall come upon 68 thee, and the power of the Most High shall overshadow thee: wherefore also that which is to be born shall be called holy, the Son of God" (Lk.1:55).

On three occasions an angel appeared to Joseph, the husband of Mary, and guided him regarding future movements. The shepherds who were keeping night watches over their flock heard an angel declare the good tidings of great joy—"There is born to you this day in the city of David a Saviour, which is Christ the Lord" (Lk.2:11). It is doubtful if we should have realized that the words in Psalm 91:11 and 12 had a direct reference to the Lord had Satan not cited them in one of the temptations. The omission by Satan of the words "To keep Thee in all Thy ways" is not without significance. From the pinnacle of the temple the adversary challenged the Lord to demonstrate that the words in Psalm 91 applied to Him. "If Thou art the Son of God, cast Thyself down from hence" (Lk.4:9). The Lord's reply was: "Again it is written, Thou shalt not tempt the Lord thy God (Matt.4:7). When the devil had completed every temptation "angels came and ministered unto Him" (Matt.4:11).

The three synoptic Gospels describe the scene in the garden of Gethsemane, and each writer testifies to the sorrow and deep distress of the Lord: "O My Father, if it be possible, let this cup pass away from Me: nevertheless, not as I will, but as Thou wilt" (Matt.26:39). At this crucial juncture we read, "And there appeared unto Him an angel from heaven, strengthening Him" (Lk.22:43). Following His arrest some of the disciples were prepared to defend the Lord, and indeed Simon Peter drew a sword and cut off the right ear of Malchus, the servant of the high priest. The Lord's response was, "Thinkest thou that I cannot beseech My Father, and He shall even now send Me more than twelve legions of angels? How then should the Scriptures be fulfilled, that thus is must be?" (Matt.26:53,54).

No letter in the New Testament refers more touchingly to the sufferings of the Christ than the apostle Peter's first letter. He describes himself as a witness of the sufferings of Christ. There were others deeply concerned regarding Christ's sufferings. We read in 1 Peter 1:12, "which things angels desire to look into." The Greek word 'parakupto' corresponds to the phrase "to look into." Dr. Young defines this word as "to stoop alongside of." This definition suggests that angels looked on in wonder and amazement at the happenings at

Golgotha, and wished to probe the mystery. It may on the other hand suggest that angels waited anxiously for the word of command to go to the help of their Lord, but that command was never given. An angel rolled away the stone from the mouth of the tomb and declared the glorious fact, "He is not here; for He is risen." At the ascension of the Lord two men in white apparel declared to the disciples, "This Jesus, which was received up from you into heaven, shall so come in like manner as ye beheld Him going into heaven" (Acts 1:11). We have traced the part played by angels from the birth of the Lord Jesus until He was received back to the Father's right hand.

Angels and the book of the Revelation

The fact has already been mentioned that angels are referred to some 68 times in this book, and readers will readily observe that they play an important role. Attention is now drawn to some of these instances. The Revelation was sent and signified by an angel. Each letter to the seven churches is addressed to the angel (or messenger) of the church. It was a strong angel who proclaimed the question, "Who is worthy to open the book, and to loose the seals thereof?" (Rev.5:2) . One hundred million, and thousands of thousands of angels raise their voices, "Worthy is the Lamb that hath been slain."

In chapter 7 we see four angels holding the four winds of the earth and another angel restrained them with the words, "Hurt not the earth, neither the sea, nor the trees, till we have sealed the servants of our God on their foreheads." Seven angels with seven trumpets are mentioned in chapter 8:2, and the blowing of these trumpets and subsequent events are described in chapters 8, 9 and 11. We must not overlook the strong angel with the little book open, standing upon the sea and the earth mentioned in chapter 10. The victory of Michael and his angels over Satan and his angels results in Satan and his angels being cast down to the earth. In chapter 14 there are four angels each with a message, and in the following chapters there are seven angels with seven plagues which are the last, for in them is finished the wrath of God. An angel having great authority and another strong angel who cast a millstone into the sea are mentioned in chapter 18, while in the next chapter we have an angel standing in the sun. The key of the abyss and a great chain are used by an angel to bind the Devil and cast him into the abyss for a thousand 70 years. Finally, "One of the seven angels who had the seven bowls, who were laden with the seven last plagues; and he spake with me, saying, Come hither, I will shew thee the Bride, the wife of the Lamb" (Rev.21:9).

18

DIVINE CONTROL AND HUMAN AUTHORITY IN WORLD AFFAIRS (CLIVE BISHOP)

Two related concepts pervade the Bible; on the one hand the sovereignty of God, and on the other the freedom and accountability of man. The Bible maintains that God is sovereign and controls all things so that they are directed ultimately to His glory (Eph.1:11). Scripture, with its particular reference to man, reveals God's determined and unchangeable plan for his redemption, resulting in the overthrow of the forces of evil which oppose God (Rev.19ff) and brought about man's fall, and culminating in God's intention to consummate all in Christ (Phil.2:9-11). This plan belongs to the eternal counsels of the omnipotent God, and derives from an unseen order unknown, except by divine revelation, on earth.

It is central to this concept that events are neither indeterminate nor random in this great strategy of the ages. The Bible maintains equally that man has the power of unconstrained and responsible choice for the consequence of which he is accountable. Man is a physical, temporal and spiritual being whose primary frame of reference is the physical universe of which he is a part. To him the future is largely unpredictable and indeterminate (Prov.27:1; Eccl.9) , and so there is an apparent conflict between this fact of human experience and the revealed concept of a determinate and unalterable plan emanating from God who controls all things, causing even the free acts of men to work together for His purposes (e. g. Gen.45:8). Scripture nowhere attempts a reconciliation of the two concepts; they are presented as separate and equally acceptable statements.

The source of the apparent conflict is the attempted comparison of the two concepts with quite disparate frames of reference. The Bible maintains that human affairs are under control. Some have sought reconciliation, arguing that events are indeterminate, and without definable direction or end; or else alleging that a deterministic arrangement absolves man from responsibility and frees him to live as he likes. It is only by faith in the grace of God that we can accept the two concepts simultaneously, and that they meet in the person of His Son, the Lord Jesus Christ. In Him the eternal and the temporal are conjoined so that God's plan of salvation could be accomplished and opportunity given to man, by his choice, to have a part in the eternal life Christ has purchased.

In the book of Revelation God, by His grace, and through the opening of the seven seals, has revealed some future events, and they are presented in the spiritual frame of reference. Divine control affects both individuals and also the nations of which they are part. Revelation outlines the events leading to the ultimate overthrow of evil. The alliances and actions of nations illustrate "that the Most High ruleth in the kingdom of men, and giveth it to whomsoever He will, and setteth up over it the lowest of men" (Dan.4:17). Nations comprise people who are free to give assent either willingly or by coercion to the ruling power or person, or to dissent. Both free choice by the ballot box and the totalitarian system conform equally to the constraints of Acts 17:26. The rulers of the nations are entrusted with authority and, as men, they exercise it within the temporal reference frame and, like all men, are accountable to God for their actions. They are under the control of God whether they willingly acknowledge His sovereignty or whether through ignorance or in defiance they are unaware of, or deny, His sovereignty.

Even to the most powerful of men, such as the beast, the future is largely un-predictable, but his actions, though wholly directed against God, nevertheless are ordained so as to do His will. It is instructive in this connection to note how often expressions like "it was given unto them" are used in Revelation (e.g. 6:4,8; 9:3, 4; 13:5,7) 15; 17:17). Of these Revelation 17:17 demonstrates that in the future, as in the past, individuals with freedom of choice agree in support of a ruler (here the beast) who is under the control of God. Though it might appear that human affairs are from time to time under the control of the malevolent power of Satan, and in particular that in Revelation 13:2 the beast receives his authority from the Dragon, it is clear that he is no more than de facto ruler, as Job 1:12 and 2:6 indicate. The nations too are under the control of God, whether willingly as were Israel in the Old Testament (Ex.19:8) and as God's people are today or, as the Gentile nations, in ignorance or defiance.

Revelation describes the oppression of Israel by the Gentile nations and is consistent with the mutual antipathy that has long been between them. Their antipathy is ordained of God. The rise of Babylon as a world power coincided with the fall of Jerusalem. The despot Nebuchadnezzar is described as "My servant" (Jer.25:9ff), and the way in which Babylon served the purposes of God is expanded in Ezek.29:17-20. The end of the Babylonian empire similarly coincided with the return to Jerusalem of the remnant of Ezra 1. These events presage the time of the end in which the oppression of Israel by the Gentiles during the Great Tribulation is the prelude to the establishment of the millennial kingdom with Israel as its centre. The nations who follow the beast are judged by the Lord Jesus Christ after their defeat at Armageddon.

By contrast Israel, recognizing the Lord Jesus Christ as her Deliverer, is established under His control during His reign on earth. This overall control of the nations is without prejudice to the operation of human will. Perhaps the most striking example concerns the Lord Jesus Christ (Jn 11:47-53). Caiaphas had appraised the situation he faced and came to a decision. He was free to select other courses, but he chose the one in which Christ was delivered up "by the determinate counsel and foreknowledge of God" (Acts 2:23; 4:25-28). Then, as always, God's foreordained purpose was brought about despite the unfettered exercise of human authority.

19

HEAVENLY VISIONS IN REVELATION AND SCRIPTURE (NORMAN MCKAY)

God has spoken in "diverse manners" and one of them surely is the heavenly vision. Old and New Testaments contain heavenly visions and we see similarities, differences, lessons and warnings in them. For our present purpose we shall consider three men in the Old Testament and three in the New, all of whom saw heavenly visions; and we shall look at them under the headings: The Man, Main Features, The Message and The Result.

THE MAN

Let us consider Isaiah, Ezekiel, Daniel, Stephen, Paul and John.

Isaiah

The book named after this man is called "the vision of Isaiah" and for a man to receive such an account of the condition of God's people calls for real communion between heaven and earth. How close the communion was is shown in 2 Kings 20. Isaiah had just told Hezekiah that he would die and not live. He was walking towards the centre of the city when a new message came from God to Hezekiah. The secret of this communion is made plain in the

84

great heavenly vision of chapter six. Isaiah's basic humility and repentance are seen in the words: "Woe is me ... I am a man of unclean lips."

Only a humble and cleansed man could receive such a vision and transmit it to God's people. Ezekiel Here is a man who was among the captives by the river Chebar among the Lord's people. Chapter one tells us he saw visions of God and the heavens were opened. Not only is Ezekiel among the Lord's people but he, like Isaiah, also humbles himself before the glory of Jehovah and falls upon his face. Two other points to be noted are that he is called a priest, and "son of man." In the matter of communication with heaven, he is used in both directions, as priest from the people to God and as prophet from God to the people. This point, and the fact that he is called "son of man," surely lead us to the conclusion that he is a type of the Lord Himself.

Daniel

This "man of prayer" was greatly blessed with visions of God. He was of royal blood and was in Babylon with a captive nation. As in the case of Isaiah and Ezekiel, Daniel humbled himself before God and in chapter 9 says: "O Lord, hear; O Lord, forgive."

Stephen

Here was a man full of grace and power, full of faith and of the Holy Spirit. His communion with heaven and its power is seen in his works: "He wrought great wonders and signs among the people."

Paul

Unlike the others, this man is first viewed going in the wrong direction and his heavenly vision was necessary so that he could be turned around and used in the Lord's will. He was blinded and when his eyes were opened he saw nothing. He later testified that he could not see for the "glory of that light"; it blinded him for ever to earthly things and from that time onward the words were true, "For me to live is Christ."

John

An unusual case indeed, for John had personal experience with the Lord on earth before he saw the heavenly vision. In the one case he leaned on Jesus' breast but in the other, when he saw the glory, he fell at His feet as one dead. In the one case he was called "the disciple whom Jesus loved" and in the other he heard the words "Fear not, I am the First and the Last."

MAIN FEATURES

The outstanding feature in all these cases is that a Man is involved in each vision. Isaiah 53 is totally concerned with the Lord Jesus and His sacrifice. In Daniel 10 after mourning and fasting for three weeks, Daniel saw a vision of a man clothed in linen and girded with gold, surely speaking of the same Person. Ezekiel's first vision ends with a Man upon a throne and we know there is only one Man on heaven's throne. Stephen saw the Lord on the right hand of God in his glimpse into heaven. Paul saw the Lord's glory and heard his voice as well, and John's story, all 22 chapters of it, is "The Revelation of Jesus Christ."

Another feature of most of the heavenly visions is the throne. This speaks of authority and judgement. God's authority had been despised by His people. Sin and disobedience characterized them in Old Testament times and judgement was called for and prophesied as the result of the vision. The New Testament occurrences are not different in essence, Stephen saw the throne and personally bowed to the "all authority" of the One upon it. But what about those who were stoning him? They, including Saul of Tarsus, despised the name of Jesus and refused to bow to His authority. John, in his first vision, saw the Lord in glory walking in the midst of the lampstands and heard statements of authority and judgement such as: "I will remove the lampstand" and "I have this against thee."

THE MESSAGE

The prophets and apostles received a message from God which came through a vision and was to be delivered to the people. What was the message? Firstly it was a call to repentance because of their sin and rebellion. Secondly, failure to do this would result in sure and certain judgement. But the great God of mercy did not only pronounce judgement, and so thirdly, grace and mercy are considered. Part of Isaiah's wonderful vision states: "He was wounded for our transgressions," and wherever possible, God through His grace will solve the sin question. Some of the pronounced judgements of course are irreversible, such as the vision of Daniel concerning the end time when "wrath would be poured out," and John's vision of the seals being opened and the words which were written: "The great day of Their wrath is come; and who is able to stand?"

THE RESULTS

This is difficult to assess in relation to the nation of Israel and God's people in this dispensation. The effect of the vision on the person who saw it however was very real and immediate. Isaiah said, "Woe is me," and he recounted his sins and the sins of the nation. Ezekiel fell upon his face, the Spirit entered into him and he heard Him that spoke. Daniel also fell with his face to the ground and there remained no strength in him. We have already mentioned that Paul was a changed man and this caused him to glory in tribulation. John also fell at his feet as one dead and was later told to "Come up hither, and I will show thee the things which must come to pass hereafter."

Perhaps the most dramatic result was seen in Stephen's experience. After he had seen the heavenly vision he could say with the grace of the great Master Himself: "Lord, lay not this sin to their charge." We are sure that if nations had been affected in the same way as these individuals as a result of heavenly visions, it would have been a different world today. And what about us? Is there a message in these visions? Yes indeed! The One who walked amidst the lampstands is still standing with open arms saying: "Behold, I stand at the door and knock: If any man hear My voice …" Have we heard His voice? Have we responded to it? Are we supping with Him? May the visions and their message speak to all our hearts!

20

THE ANTICHRIST (TOM HOPE)

World problems today centre largely in the need to relieve international tensions and to revise the monetary system in order to provide greater economic stability. These urgent considerations call for a person strong enough to impose the necessary changes. We know that such a Person will be found when the Lord Jesus Christ comes to earth to reign for 1000 years (Rev.20:4). But the question arises, "Will this be the direct outcome of present universal problems?"

In the following comments we shall seek to show from Scripture that before that great day of peace on earth dawns, another will try to create such conditions and will fail. The Person. Men of today, educated to be specialists in every field to a standard unknown heretofore, and with technical "know-how" beyond the wildest dreams of our forefathers, cannot begin to grapple with the problems. What manner of person, therefore, will dare to cope with such a task? In the writings of Daniel much is said about this, but it is our purpose to gather our material from the New Testament.

From the outset we must clearly separate two things—the man and the spirit he embodies. In 1 John 2:18 both these are mentioned: "Antichrist cometh ... even now have there arisen many antichrists." The spirit of antichrist has been manifested down through the years, and will culminate when the Antichrist arises. He is clearly identified as an individual, being described in 2 Thess.2:3 as "the man of sin ... the son of perdition," one "whose coming is according to the working of Satan with all power and signs and lying wonders." This links up with Rev.13:4,5. "They worshipped the dragon (Satan), because he gave his authority unto the beast ... there was given to him a mouth speaking great things and blasphemies; and there was given to him authority to continue forty and two months."

So we can summarise this section as follows:

1. This will take place at the time of the end.

2. Prophecy foretells a time to come when a man is seen as head of a world system.

3. The man will be a follower and tool of Satan.

4. He will be allowed by God to have great power, but for a limited time only.

The System

1 John 2:18 confirms that there have arisen many antichrists. When the Antichrist comes, what then? His power will give him authority over ten kingdoms, either by conquest or by the rulers submitting to him. In all things he will dominate and succeed. It is suggested that a unified monetary system will reduce economic barriers and so facilitate his rise to power; also that his peace formula will reconcile even Jew and Arab for a time. He will dominate the economic scene. As today many workers are dependent on a trade union card to continue in employment, so in that day none will be able to buy or sell unless they carry on their person the mark of the beast (Rev.13:16,17).

Some will boldly show the mark, the mystic number 666, engraved on their forehead; others will carry it secretly on the palm of their hand, only to be shown or exposed in case of emergency or at will. Does this foreshadow a further extension of secret police methods? In his continued domination the Antichrist will be ably supported by his assistant, the beast of Rev.13:11. Despite his horns, this is no lamb in character, but the offspring of the dragon. Eventually this false prophet will persuade the people to "make an image to the beast" (v.15), and to worship the image. This will mark the beginning of the end. In his rise to power the Antichrist will have pacified the Jews by covenanting to allow the worship of Jehovah to continue in the land. The sacrifices of the Old Testament will again be offered in Jerusalem, and the associated Aaronic/Levitical services will be renewed. But a crisis will develop—to worship the image of the beast or die (v.15).

In their day the companions of Daniel faced a similar threat, and conquered. What will the godly Jews of that day do? They will defy the order. As a consequence their treaty will be broken, sacrifices to Jehovah will cease, the image of the beast will be set up in the Temple at Jerusalem for the peoples to see and worship, and the devout Jew will flee (see Matt.24:15-22). The great dictator will then war with and persecute the Jews for forty-two months. All nations will be drawn to do battle in Palestine against Israel, unaware that this great and final battle is set so that the purposes of God can be fulfilled. The holy city will be compassed about, and for Israel all seem lost. When we consider the instruments of war available today, what will be available in the way of armaments in that day?

His Judgement

The final overthrow of this dictator is graphically described in Rev. 19:19,20. He made war against Him that sat on the horse, the Lord Jesus Christ. As for the beast and the false prophet—"they twain were cast alive into the lake of fire that burneth with brimstone." So all the grandiose schemes of the dragon, put into execution by the beast (the Antichrist) and promoted by the false prophet, will finally collapse. His rise is sure, his time of power is sure, his ultimate end is also sure. Tension is not overcome by him despite all his power and authority. A unified system of foreign exchange does not give peace of mind to earthly peoples. He shows the ultimate folly of many antichrists, and the destruction of his government paves the way for the Prince of Peace who shall rule in righteousness.

Conclusion

As it has been from the beginning, he that opposeth God is eventually overruled by the power of the One so opposed. We see the day approaching, for who can fail to be aware of the signs of the times as we observe world events in our days, all pointing to an early fulfilment of the prophetic word? We look for the promised return of our Ruler, who will take us to be with Himself before the endtime. What manner of persons ought we to be, the more so as we see the day approaching? Our time is short, and is shortening day by day. Let us the more earnestly raise the warning cry to flee from the wrath to come! For we are assured that "the thing is established by God, and God will shortly bring it to pass."

21

SATAN'S FUTURE ROLE IN WORLD AFFAIRS (BRIAN FULLARTON)

The third chapter of the Bible records mankind's first encounter with his arch-foe, Satan, and the third from the end foretells the latter's final expulsion from the earth. He is everywhere represented as the implacable enemy of God and man. Though unable to lay claim to the three great attributes of Deity—omnipotence, omniscience and omnipresence — he is nevertheless a being of great power, having at his command mighty demoniac forces. No informed saint can think lightly of him (Jude 9).

His character is described by such significant names as "serpent" and "dragon", a roaring and ravening lion, a murderer and a liar, deceiver and seducer, tempter and accuser. Though darkness is his domain, he can appear as an "angel of light." Children of God are warned against his snares and darts, his wiles and devices. The ambitious designs of this powerful being have two main objectives. First, that he may usurp control of the nations; second, that he may introduce the false Christ, whose credentials will receive universal acceptance and who will by his feats and powers convince the most sceptical of men. The Scriptures bear evidence that the prince of this world is not complacent or satisfied with his present dominion in the lives of men. An empire on this earth, in which he is worshipped by the people and his will is acknowledged, is assuredly the plan of the master deceiver who makes war with truth, being himself the author of error.

The tragic picture of future world conditions and affairs is vividly described in chapters 6-19 of Revelation. It will be readily admitted that events mentioned can rapidly become a reality. The tremendous upheavals which have taken place in international affairs in recent times have far surpassed the predictions of shrewd minds. Man's selfish disregard for his fellows and his self-willed nature will be fully exploited by Satan to execute and hasten his sinister purposes. In chapter 6 of Revelation, while clearly the wrath of the Almighty is awakening, there can be detected movements of Satan on earth as the seals are opened by the Lamb. Revolutionary happenings begin to take place. These coincide with the prophecy of the Lord Jesus Christ in Matthew 24:1-8, in which He outlines the "beginning of travail", which will precede "the tribulation, the great one" (literal translation). In verse 2 of Revelation 6 there would appear to be the emergence of Satan's representative, one who will dominate the political scene until the whole of the revived Roman empire is firmly in his grasp. In the second seal a second rider appears bearing the emblem of war, a great sword, and the earth is deprived of peace.

Wars and rumours of wars only form the beginning of the terrible throes which will produce ever more slaughter on the earth. These are inevitable outcomes of war—famine, death, the blood of Jewish martyrs, cataclysms of astonishing proportions, terror infiltrating every stratum of society, the displacement of great rulers and leaders—to mention only a few. Behind the rising tide of travails is Satan himself. A series of divine judgements is presented by the sounding of the trumpets which would appear to be largely concurrent with the vial judgements of chapters 15 and 16. The three "Woes" (8:13) indicate the last of the trumpet soundings. In the judgements there are drastic happenings upon the earth, in the sea, in the fountains of waters and in the heavenly realms. The Woes have to do with those that "dwell on the earth." Prior to this we see the destructive agencies and powers of nature, upheavals among nations, the saturation of every department of life with poisonous elements.

Man arrives at his selected destination at last in chapter 9. 15.

In the first Woe, initiated by the fifth trumpet sound, the apostle discerns a great fallen being to whom extraordinary power is given— a star fallen from heaven, to whom was given the key of the abyss (9.:1). His league with the king of the abyss, Satan himself (verse 11), together with his tremendous diabolical powers, leave no doubt as to his identity as the antichrist (2 Thess.2:9). His character is amplified in the second beast of Revelation 13. [See Editorial Note below.] This counterfeit saviour will release demoniac forces from the depths of the abyss. Earth's inhabitants will find themselves so sorely perplexed that life will become unbearable, yet escape will be denied them (9:6). The locust, the scorpion and the war-horse conjure a terrifying picture of the power of their king, whose name in Hebrew, "Abaddon", means Destroyer. These are probably the deceiving spirits and teachings of demons, speaking lies in hypocrisy.

The second Woe introduces armies of staggering proportions (two hundred million) invading with equipment of death which, together with the other two Woes, results in the third part of men being killed. This is all occasioned by the sins that have perverted civilization. These are given in detail to show the vile desires and abhorrent depravities to which man has bowed. The third Woe, which begins after the resurrection and ascension of the two witnesses, and the earthquake which results in the death of seven thousand (11:13) brings the Judge of all the earth to the earth. How characteristic of God that, at this early stage in the vision, at such a dark period on the earth, there is given the reassurance of the control which He exercises in spite of prevailing evils in the world! In chapters 12-19 of Revelation, the details of what has been a panoramic view are now brought under closer examination.

The spotlight of inspiration is on the second half of Daniel's seventieth week, where we view the very height of Satan's evil. John is to prophesy again concerning peoples, nations and many kings (10:77). In Rev. 12 there appear the final stages in man's rebellion against God and in his manipulation by

Satan. This being will be at his most powerful as political, religious and diabolical forces thoroughly corrupt the whole earth. He knows his sphere is limited to earth and sea; his time short; therefore, his wrath is great. The systematizing of evil doctrine and practice will be rife.

The character of Satan looms large in chapter 12, cruel and loathsome, subtle, a slanderer and adversary, the relentless opponent of God and man. The believer's only recourse is to the blood of the Lamb and His testimony. The prince of death can never bear any reminder of the victory of the Prince of life and glory. The increased sorrow and woe on earth will therefore be brought about by the humiliation of Satan and the realization of his limited time. The exalted Saviour, of course, is the object of the serpent's hatred. This angry adversary will make his fiercest assault during the latter half of the seven-year period. The beasts seen emerging from the land and sea (Rev.13:1,11) reveal Satan's political genius. The first beast receives the power, throne and authority of the great red dragon. The second beast bears the similitude of the first (13:12). Satan will make full use of these instruments to lead world nations into unity, albeit short-lived.

The final state of Gentile domination on the earth is the ten-kingdom confederacy, and a study of Daniel 2 shows the answer of the image in the beast of Revelation 13. The description of the beast's features make it clear that it will be a despotic regime. He will blaspheme against God, His Name, His tabernacle and heavendwellers (13:5). The second beast of Revelation 13:11 is referred to in chapters 19 and 20 as the false prophet. This great person makes his appearance from the earth and co-operates with the political leader. Thus Rome and Jerusalem enter into a pact. Satan again is at work behind the scenes as the character of this beast is both lamb-like and lion-like. Qualities calculated to deceive and make him totally acceptable in the religious realm (13:13) are apparent. His influence as antichrist will stretch into the revived Roman empire.

The very same spirit which cast the nation of Israel into blindness as to the real Messiah now assumes control again in their falling a prey to the wiles of this master deceiver. His ability to bring fire from heaven, and his successful image of the first beast and giving breath to it, will prove him to be the Christ in the eyes of the people. [See Editorial Note below.] The man of sin will eventually find his place in the new temple at Jerusalem and the climax will be reached when he sets himself up as God. This will be the fulfilment of Daniel's prediction of the "abomination of desolation" (Dan.9:27). In view of all this, it is easy to visualize this great religious deceiver enforcing the mark on the right hand or forehead (13:16) as essential for commercial transactions. Obviously, there is a marriage of religion and commerce here. The "mystery of lawlessness" was already in operation in the time of the apostle Paul in preparation for the revelation of the "lawless one" (2 Thess.2:7). John himself spoke of those who denied the actual incarnation of Christ (1 Jn 2:22).

Truly, the perfect atmosphere exists for Satan's presentation of the travesty of our great God and Saviour, Jesus Christ. That system of politics and religion combined, the Great Harlot, Mystery, Babylon the Great, suffers a great downfall and the instruments of her ruin are her own devotees (17:16-18). Satan, the beast and the false prophet, the evil trinity, together with their minions, suffer defeat at the hand of the Lamb. (17:14). The grievous evils of these betrayers of mankind are mentioned again in Revelation 19. The two lieutenants of Satan are committed alive into the "lake of fire that burneth with brimstone."

Thus end all Satan's designs to usurp the prerogatives of God and of His Christ. He himself is committed to the abyss for 1, 000 years. This powerful intelligence rises again to lead Gog and Magog (Ezek.38-39; Rev.20:8) to inevitable wrath. The lake of fire which he shares with his confederates, becomes his place of eternal dwelling.

Editorial Note on the Two Beasts of Rev. 14.

The writer of the foregoing article is among those who identify the antichrist with the second beast of Rev. 13. However, editors consider antichrist to be the first beast (Rev. 13. 1). A resume of the reasons for this view is set out below:

(1) Prophetic scriptures describe an outstandingly wicked dictator who rules prior to the coming of the Son of Man. He is variously described as: (a) The little horn (Dan.7:8, 11, 23-26, 8:9-12); (b) The prince that shall come (Dan.9:26); (c) The king of the north (Dan.11.30-45); (d) The abomination of desolation (Matt.24:75); (e) The man of sin (2 Thess.2:3-10); (f) The antichrist (1 Jn 2:18-23; 2 Jn 7); (g) The beast (Rev.13:1-10).

Extreme manifestations of boasting, lying and blasphemy are described in these scriptures, and what is most remarkable is the highhanded manner in which this ruler is said in some of the accounts to interfere with the temple services and put himself in the place of God. What greater lie is there than to impersonate God? The antichrist, who is the arch liar and deceiver (2 Jn 7), is thus to be identified with the man of sin, who "sitteth in the temple of God setting himself forth as God" (2 Thess.2:3,4). The other references in Daniel, Matthew and Revelation 13. 1-10 describe a man so similar in character, accomplishments and timing to the man of sin that there seems no alternative but to accept their identity with him and thus with antichrist.

2. Mr. J. Miller says, "The rise of the beast from the abyss is no ordinary happening. The beast, who is also the antichrist, after dying will rise from the dead, and in him there will be an imitation of the real Christ. Some have thought and taught that the antichrist is the second beast of Revelation 13. This is quite incorrect. The second beast is not slain: he has no deathstroke, he is not worshipped, but encourages with all the powers at his disposal the worship of the first beast. Some have claimed as proof of their view that the Jews would not accept a Gentile king as their Messiah and therefore the first beast, being a Gentile king, would be unacceptable. But there is nothing in this chapter or any other in Scripture to prove that the first beast is a Gentile, and the second, a false prophet, is a Jew.

What is there to hinder the first beast being a Jew by race? Indeed we do not know that the seven kings follow each other by heredity. They may be elected to the office of kings of Babylon. Ezekiel 21:25 gives help in this matter of the beast, who is the antichrist: 'And thou, O deadly wounded wicked one, the prince of Israel, whose day is come, in the time of the iniquity of the end.' The prince of Israel is the deadly wounded one, which I take to mean, the beast with the death stroke."

3. It may be argued that, since it is the false prophet who works the signs to deceive men, he is the son of perdition of 2 Thessalonians 2, whose coming is "according to the working of Satan with all power and signs and lying wonders." We do not consider this reasoning to be sound because the signs are said to accompany the son of perdition, not to be actually executed by him.

22

DIVINE JUDGEMENT THROUGH THE SON (LESLEY HICKLING)

In the synagogue at Nazareth the Lord Jesus opened the book that was given to Him and read from the prophecy of Isaiah concerning Himself (Lk.4:16). He read of the great work He had come to do, to bring good tidings to the poor, to proclaim release to the captives, give sight to the blind and bring liberty to the bruised. Then He closed the book and sat down without finishing the paragraph. The phrase "and the day of vengeance of our God" was left unread. For God sent not His Son into the world to judge the world; but that the world should be saved through Him (Jn3:17).

We delight to think of the gracious work that He came to do, and of God's mercy and love manifest in His Son. But the last phrase of the verse is none the less true and Scripture is not silent on this aspect of His character. The Father "gave Him authority to execute judgement, because He is the Son of Man" (Jn 5:27). This is He which is ordained of God to be the Judge of quick and dead (Acts 10:42). God is righteous and must judge. In this article we consider briefly this aspect of His work. His message to the Churches John, in the Spirit on the Lord's Day, saw a vision that made a profound impression upon him; One with feet as of burnished brass and eyes as a flame of fire. He stood in the midst of the churches. Everything that was going on there was seen by Him who alone could assess its value in truth and righteousness.

In Ephesus He saw their toil and patience and their hatred of evil men, but He also saw the lack of fire of first love motivating their works. He saw the saints in Pergamum holding fast in difficult circumstances but tolerating those who propagated false teaching. In Thyatira He saw those increasing in works which He approved but failing to judge the woman who seduced the saints. And so on. Each was brought under the searchlight of the True and Righteous One. Their works were reviewed and they were warned of the consequences of failure to respond to the message He had sent to them. They had a responsibility to hear and to act lest His judgement fall upon them. His judgement of the works of believers Believers look forward to the time when the shout of the Lord will call them away from the impediments of earth to meet the Lord in the air.

But then, too, the last opportunity of earthly service will have passed and we shall face the great assessment of our works. Saved eternally as to our persons we must nevertheless appear before the judgement-seat of Christ to receive the rewards of our works. "We must all be made manifest before the judgement-seat of Christ" (2 Cor.5:10). No exceptions here; we must all be made manifest. But, each one shall give account of himself (Rom.14:12). What an intensely personal thing this is! All the things we have done in the body made manifest before Him as He assesses, in truth and righteousness, of what sort they are. How little may remain of some of those acts of which we thought so highly and how much more may count those things that seemed less to us but were done out of a purer motive for Him! Well may we consider now, ... when in His Holy presence, We again our works shall meet, Will they stand the fiery testing Of the coming judgement-seat?

God's judgements in the earth

Men go on in rebellion against God, resisting Him or denying His existence and ordering their lives without reference to His laws. But God is in control and men will be brought to know it. John is given a vision (Rev.5) of God's book of judgement, written within and on the back. Who is worthy to open it? Only the One whom men despised, but to whom God committed all judgement. "I saw in the midst of the throne ... a Lamb standing, as though it had been, slain ... and He came, and He taketh it out of the right hand of Him that sat on the throne" (Rev.5:6,7). As the seals are opened earth is smitten with a period of unprecedented tribulation and men begin to taste the judgements of a righteous God. At this time the sinister figure of the great world dictator arises, with Satanic power, speaking great things and blasphemies and achieving authority over every tribe and tongue and people and nation. In his hatred of God he gathers together earth's armies in an imposing array of military might against Him that is called Faithful and True.

This is the one who stood in the synagogue at Nazareth as He continues to fulfil the prophecy He started reading there and to proclaim the day of vengeance of our God. His eyes are as a flame of fire and a sharp sword proceeds out of His mouth. Men are killed by it and earth's armies cannot stand before the might of the King of kings and Lord of lords. By His authority the Beast and his prophet are cast into the lake of fire and Satan is consigned to the abyss. What a fearful picture of the Lord Jesus as He rides out in judgement! The judgement of the nations Thus the Lord comes to the earth and Matthew 25 makes it clear that all nations who are then living on the earth will be brought before Him to be judged in righteousness on the basis of their works and their attitude to His people. The Lord will separate them; some on His right hand to enter into the kingdom and some on His left to depart into the eternal fire. There will be no appeal in this judgement. All judgement is in His hand.

The judgement of Gog and Magog

Even after the righteous rule of the Lord Jesus for a thousand years men will still be capable of lending an ear to the great deceiver when he is released from his prison. By him they will be gathered to make war with the saints. But no fighting is necessary in this battle. Upon them the judgement of God will speedily descend as "fire came down out of heaven, and devoured them"

(Rev.20:9). The great white throne judgement In a few brief phrases the divine revelation describes the last great tribunal at the end of time when the rest of the dead are raised and called to stand before the judgement throne. The books are opened and the dead are judged out of the things written in the books. Here all men of all time stand accountable to the Judge of all the earth and "if any was not found written in the book of life, he was cast into the lake of fire." Thus in the unfolding of the Scripture we behold the goodness and severity of God. In the proper time in the working out of God's purposes the whole of the prophecy from Isaiah sees its fulfilment.

23

THE NATIONS—AT THE END TIME; IN THE MILLENNIUM; IN ETERNITY (R. LINDSAY)

AT THE END TIME

1) The Western Empire

Central to any study of the End Times must be an understanding of the spiritual symbolism of Daniel's dream (Dan.7). Arising out of the sea, Daniel saw four beasts. The first was like a lion, and had eagle's wings; the second was a bear, raised up on one side; the third as a winged leopard with four heads; and the fourth was a nondescript beast. It was terrible, powerful and exceedingly strong. But its most remarkable feature lay in its horns. There were ten of them—and, in addition, there arose yet another horn, a little one, before which three of the existing horns were plucked up by the roots. So this "little horn" became dominant; it had remarkable eyes, and a mouth speaking great things.

Most commentators are agreed that these beasts represent world-empires.

The lion was symbolic of the Chaldean empire; the bear of the Medo-Persians; the leopard of the Greek empire of Alexander the Great; and the final beast spoke of the Roman empire. This interpretation also applies to the four stages of the image Nebuchadnezzar saw in his dream in Daniel 2. A study of the fourth empire, in Daniel 2 and 7, leads to the conclusion that certain of the details (e. g. the rise of the little horn) 101 have not been seen in past history, and that the Roman empire must still have a part to play in future world events. This is confirmed by the vision given to John (Revelation 13:1-10) of the beast which came out of the sea, having seven heads and ten horns. Evidently, John's vision was of the same power as Daniel saw, and from both visions we learn that, unlike the other three, the Roman empire is not yet finished. It will reappear, in the end times, as a federation of ten kingdoms. There has, of course, been speculation as to which grouping of nations is referred to.

Some have seen a "United States of Europe" as the coming Roman revival. Others have different thoughts. What is certain, however, is that the dominant personality of this coming Confederation will be the ruler represented by the "little horn" in Daniel's vision. Not one of the original ten, he arises and violently puts down three of them, establishing himself as the undisputed leader. Clearly, he will be a man of magnetic personality, and of remarkable economic and political skills. Variously he is described as Antichrist (1 Jn 2:18); the Man of Sin, the Son of perdition (2 Thess.2:3); and the Lawless One (2 Thess.2:8). As his lieutenant, Antichrist will have one described by John as "another beast" (Rev.13:11) and as "the false prophet" (Rev.19:20). The activities of these two evil individuals throughout the period of Daniel's 70th week have been the subject of much comment in this year, all consideration leading up to their destruction at Armageddon by Israel's Redeemer.

The Kings of the North and South

The great western empire under Antichrist will not be alone on the prophetic stage at this time. Daniel 11:40 introduces us to two more kingdoms, represented by the King of the South (Egypt?) and the King of the North. Who this latter king was is not clearly determined. Some students suggest he may be King of Syria. Others, looking to Ezekiel 38, see Gog, Prince of Rosh, and references to "the uttermost parts of the north" as indication that this northern kingdom may be Russia. Current events may well lend support to this view. [The other view advanced elsewhere is that Antichrist is himself the "King of the North"—Editors]

The Nations from the East

Revelation 16:12 gives us an insight into yet another group of nations. When John saw the sixth vial of Divine wrath poured out, it was upon the Euphrates, the waters of which dried up to make ready the way for the kings that come from the sunrising. Waves of eastern invaders shall enter Israel's land, drawn, as are the others "unto the war of the great day of God, the Almighty" (Revelation 16:14). 4)

Armageddon

Thus, Israel shall once again become the arena of the world, invaded on all sides. But, in her darkest hour, Heaven will open and her Redeemer will appear, sitting upon a white horse and followed by the armies of heaven. Out of His mouth will proceed a sharp sword, with which to smite the armies of the nations. At the sight of Him, the Beast and the kings of the earth with their armies will unite to make war against Him, little recognising that God has brought them together to this day of cataclysmic judgement. At Har-Magedon the battle will be joined. It will be brief, but terrible, for the Lord Jesus "treadeth the winepress of the fierceness of the wrath of Almighty God."

The Beast and his false prophet will be taken, and cast into the lake of fire. The armies of the nations shall be utterly devastated, and the birds will sate themselves on the flesh of the slain. For Israel, it will be a glorious deliverance, at the hands of Him whom they have pierced; for Antichrist and the nations, a day of fierce judgement by the One against whom they had so arrogantly set themselves.

The Valley of Jehoshaphat

Yet a further judgement remains to be executed upon the living nations. They will be gathered to the Valley of Jehoshaphat (Joel 3:12), and there the Son of Man shall sit on the throne of His glory, and shall separate them one from another, as the shepherd separateth the sheep from the goats. (Matt.25:31,32). Some will enter His millennial kingdom, while others will be consigned to eternal punishment.

IN THE MILLENNIUM

Following the final destruction of the Beast and his armies at Har-Magedon, Satan will be bound for 1, 000 years, during which time he will be languishing in the abyss, "that he should deceive the nations no more, until the thousand years should be finished" (Rev.20:3). The Lord Jesus will reign over the earth and establish His universal Kingdom of righteousness. It will be a time of unparalleled blessing for all nations. In the Millennium, the nations will recognise that God has glorified Jerusalem and exalted His people. From all nations, men shall come to do service for Israel, and "all that see them shall acknowledge them, that they are the seed which the LORD has blessed" (Is.61:9). In that day the wealth of the earth shall be poured into Israel (Is.60:11).

A notable feature of the millennial period will be the willingness of the Gentile nations to "go up to the mountain of the LORD, and to the house of the God of Jacob" (Micah 4:2), resulting in a constant stream of pilgrims to Jerusalem, where they shall share in the worship of the Lord. Despite the binding of Satan and the Lord's rule of righteousness, sin can still be detected in the millennial state (Is.65:20). Thus when, according to divine purpose, Satan will, at the conclusion of the thousand years, be released "for a little time," he shall once again be able to deceive the nations which are in the four corners of the earth, and shall lead them in one final assault on the beloved city. Those who follow him will be destroyed by fire from heaven (Rev.20:9) and Satan himself will be taken and cast into the lake of fire for ever.

IN THE ETERNAL STATE

The new earth will also have its nations. But now there will be no more sin, and the nations through all eternity will find their fulfilment in the service of God. They shall walk in the light of the holy city, and into it they shall bring their glory (Rev.21:24). From the leaves of the tree of life the nations will find their healing. Thus, throughtout the eternal ages, all nations will find their existence centred on the City of God, in the midst of which will be the throne of God and of the Lamb.

24

REVELATION—THE FITTING COMPLETION OF THE WRITTEN WORD
(A.B. ROBERTSON)

One of the most remarkable things about God's word, delivered over many hundreds of years, is how much of His purposes and plans for all of time are revealed to men. The things revealed can be outside our personal place in the time scale, but are answers to questions natural to men at any point in time. We should be left with many troublesome queries did the Bible not contain a book dealing with the final kingdom, final judgements, the exposure and destruction of forces shown to have been long in revolt against God and righteousness, the dissolution of the old earth and the establishing of the new.

The place for such a book is at the end of the Bible, for, difficult as much of the Revelation is, it would be incomprehensible had we not read our way through the other books; and except for a curiosity about the future we should not have the question seeking the answers. It takes the rest of the Bible to introduce and describe the various personalities and forces concerned with time, and the final solutions affecting them are only in place in the last book of the sixty-six. From our reading of the other books there is a certain inevitability about the broad outline of some of the Revelation, but, as with the rest of the

Bible, so much detail in presentation argues that this could only have come from the mind of God Himself. This last book is the naturally concluding communication of God with men in time.

Although a similar book could have a logical place at the end of the Old Testament, it would only be a partial answer to Jewish questions, and would have been too narrowly based. In any case, as time has gone on Israel's affairs have become interwoven in the divine pattern for all of men and all of time. Daniel and Zechariah share subjects with the Revelation, but it is only possible nearer the end of time for God to reveal His universal solutions to human history's problems, since they involve the ending of earth and time. The natural place for the record of scenes describing the conclusion of time is the last book, and anything else would interrupt the easy flow of order in divine revelation. It is exciting to find so much that concerns our Lord Himself in the Revelation, and in such circumstances as could be understood in the last book. He who said in John 14:26 of the Holy Spirit "He shall teach you all things, and bring to your remembrance all that I said unto you," makes a last dramatic intervention when speaking to the churches.

Such was the emergency and so great His personal concern that He permitted John to see Him in all His glorious state and in supreme authority. As these were certainly to be His very last words for John to report, He reminds John that He IS—nothing has changed! The description of Himself is intended to confirm and establish all already known—the faithful Witness, the Firstborn from the dead, our great Lover and Redeemer, the One with the power to make a kingdom, a priesthood and who, in the ultimate, has the keys of death and Hades. It is salutary that in the concluding book of the Bible we see Him knowing and caring about individual churches, and anxious that they should know from Himself that He is living, powerful and deeply interested in individuals.

That God is worshipped continuously by great and wonderful beings is the scene from eternity, but the opening of the books so long sealed is at the end of time, and fitting material for the last book of the Bible. The Lion of the tribe of Judah, the Root of David, is shown to be the Lamb that has been slain. He is the great and longed-for Conqueror. We have read the Gospels and the prophets, seen the despised Man and His disciples, and now this last view is of Him receiving power, riches, wisdom, might, honour, glory and blessing "for ever and ever". Naturally this revelation of the Father's intention for the Lord Jesus is in this last book for the scenes precede and introduce the end of time. He who receives the kingdom does so to take control, and He who had been meek and humiliated now initiates the great day of wrath and judgement. Paul had said in Acts 17:31, "He hath appointed a day in the which He will judge the world in righteousness by the Man whom He hath ordained"—and in this last book we see it happening and the Man is revealed.

The questions asked regarding the future for men and time are fittingly answered in this last book, and the denouncements are awesome to contemplate. God's revelation of things long sought by men and withheld till now shows a progressive deterioration of earthly conditions and associated human disasters. In all this He is merciful to some and they will find peace and plenty in the kingdom of the Lamb. He will be their Shepherd. The days of Satanic influence are shown to have their limits, and this book, expanding on other scriptural comments, details the last increase, imprisonment and eternal banishment of the great adversary. The last days grow darker for men, and events are shown to be beyond human control. Dissensions divide and confound men and their best purposes and hopes are upset. Before the awfulness of the end-time scenes men are shown to diminish—only God is in control.

Destruction of false religion, the confounding of human ingenuity in world politics, the confrontation of the armed might of men, the judgement on every rebellious system, the White Throne examination of individuals out of all of time—these are fitting subjects for the last book of the Bible. So too is the information that there is to be a continuation of divine favour and mercy towards those who trust Him in the news of a new heaven and earth.

Through all, the Lamb is magnified and honoured, seen enthroned and active. This last book establishes His triumph for ever, first in the old, and then in the new earth and heaven. These last scenes show Him pre-eminent, and God's ways and righteousness eternally established. The revelation of the Lamb in triumph belongs to these last days and when He takes control events follow each other swiftly through the deepening darkness into the brilliance of the eternal day. In all this "His servants shall do Him service"—glorious confirmation of all we could have dared to hope for.

God's promises are sure, and with the confidence this last book gives us we can join with John in his "Come, Lord Jesus." The happy anticipation this book stirs in us makes us happy that our Bible ends with such a book— a fitting completion to the written Word.

II

THE SEVEN CHURCHES OF REVELATION
(GEORGE PRASHER)

25

SEVEN GOLDEN LAMPSTANDS

Our glorified Saviour and Lord was deeply interested in the seven churches of God in the Roman province of Asia. The apostle John was instructed by the Lord to write what he saw in a book and send it to the seven churches in that province: Ephesus, Smyrna, Pergamum, Thyatira, Sardis, Philadelphia and Laodicea. "Write therefore," the Lord said, "the things which thou sawest, and the things which are, and the things which shall come to pass hereafter" (Rev.1:19).

What John had seen was the vision of the Lord Jesus, walking among the seven golden lampstands with seven stars in His right hand. "The things which are" refer to what the Lord had to say about the condition of these seven churches, as recorded in the second and third chapters of Revelation. "The things which shall come to pass hereafter" are dealt with from chapter four onward - far-reaching prophecies of a time yet future. This period, described by Daniel as "the time of the end" (Dan.11:35), will be after the Church which is Christ's Body has been taken from this world to be with Christ, when iniquity will reach its awful climax.

Our special concern in this part of the book is to learn from the Lord's messages to the churches concerning their spiritual condition - "the things which are." The coming of Christ to the air for His Church is a great landmark of divine purpose which will bring to a close this age of grace. Each believer should live daily in anticipation of this "blessed hope" being fulfilled. Until that coming we have the opportunity to carry out our Master's command to make disciples, baptizing and teaching them to observe all that He has commanded. In the first century the apostles' obedience to that command brought disciples together to form churches of God in many areas.

Seven of those churches were in the Roman province of Asia in what is now western Turkey. The first three chapters of Revelation show us how much these churches meant to the Lord Jesus; He was deeply concerned for their well-being and continuance. Still today the Holy Spirit is stirring disciples of Christ to be together to express His will as they serve in churches of God. From a study of the early part of the book of Revelation we can learn a great deal about the spiritual dangers which may spoil the effectiveness of our service for Christ. We may take to heart His analysis of the condition of those churches; we can then imitate what He commended and beware of what He condemned. "The things which are," as described in the messages to the seven churches, have special relevance to our present service for Christ; they contain valuable truth for our time.

It is of special interest that each of the seven churches was represented as a lampstand. Several older English versions of Scripture have the word "candlestick" instead of lampstand, but this was an inaccurate translation. The lampstand is a familiar scriptural symbol. For instance, God gave Moses the pattern of the golden lampstand to be used in the Tabernacle. Zechariah the prophet was given a vision of a lampstand all of gold, representing the testimony of God's people when they returned from Babylon to rebuild the Temple in Jerusalem.

Why was each church of God in apostolic times likened to a golden lampstand? It was because each was a unit of divine testimony in its local setting, whether in Ephesus, Smyrna or elsewhere. The gold reminds us that each was of divine origin. Churches of God were not the product of humanly-designed religion.

They were the result of divine revelation to the apostles, so that the will of Christ was expressed by His disciples in their principles of gathering, worship and witness. Each church was to function in the energy of the Spirit of God, illustrated by the pure olive oil of the lamps. Personal testimony has its own great value; but the full development of God's purpose in our lives demands that individual lamps should be on the lampstand, shining together for Christ.

Each local church of God has of course its God-given responsibilities, just as each lampstand stood on its own base. Yet New Testament churches of God were not independent of each other, as can be seen from a number of scriptures. The point is confirmed by the fact that John was told to write what he saw in a book and send the book to the seven churches. There were not seven books. The one book included a special message for each church, but all the messages were to be read in every church. They were mutually responsible to consider what the Lord had to say about the state of all seven churches; because they formed a united Fellowship of churches, and what affected one would have its effect upon all. Seven times in chapters 2 and 3 of Revelation the Lord repeated these words: "He that hath an ear, let him hear what the Spirit saith to the churches." In this sense they were also addressed as a whole.

The Lord Jesus was seen by John to have seven stars in His right hand. Verse 20 of chapter 1 explains: "The mystery of the seven stars which thou sawest in My right hand ... the seven stars are the angels of the seven churches." The Greek word 'angelos' is variously translated as angel or messenger according to the context. In this case it is suggested that the seven stars stood for a faithful representative of each church, upon whom the Lord knew He could rely to speak His word. The seven stars are described as being in the Lord's hand (v.16) and upon His right hand (v.20 RV margin), as though He had opened His hand to show them to John. How valuable to our Master when His servants are "in His hand," available to be used by Him as He directs!

An important point emerges in connection with the seven golden lampstands which represented the seven churches in Asia. We know that just a few decades earlier there had been a Church of God in Colossae, which was also in the Roman province of Asia. To the disciples forming that church Paul had written his wonderful epistle which forms part of our New Testament. In Revelation there is no mention of Colossae; for some reason the Church of God there must have ceased during the intervening years. Perhaps the false teaching of which Paul had warned the Colossians in his letter to them had gained a stronger grip and destroyed the church.

Whatever the reason, there was no longer a golden lampstand of divine testimony in Colossae; reminding us that churches of God are vulnerable to Satan's attacks. Only by maintaining the truths of the Faith and serving out of true love to Christ can they continue to enjoy the Lord's recognition. This is one of the clear distinctions between the believer's membership of the Church which is Christ's Body, and the disciple's place in a church of God. It is Christ Himself who baptizes the believer in one Spirit into one Body, and that can never be reverse (1 Cor.12:13). A believer may, however, be put away from a church of God for immoral conduct, false doctrine or the like. A church of God may also cease to be recognized by God as a golden lampstand because of its spiritual failure (Rev.2:5).

THE PATTERN OF THE LORD'S MESSAGE TO THE CHURCHES

A study of chapters 2 and 3 of Revelation will reveal that the messages from the Lord Jesus to each of the seven Churches of God in the Roman province of Asia follow an interesting pattern.

First, the Lord clearly identifies Himself to each Church - usually by reference to some feature of the vision in which He had manifested His glory to the apostle John. For instance, to the Church in Ephesus He introduces Himself as "He that holdeth the seven stars in His right hand"; to the Church in Smyrna, "These things saith the First and the Last, which was dead, and lived again"; to Thyatira, "These things saith the Son of God, who hath His eyes like a flame of fire, and His feet are like unto burnished brass," the important point being that as they heard the Lord's message read from the book, the disciples in each church of God would be impressed that it was the Lord Himself who was speaking to their hearts. As we read God's Word we should cultivate the attitude of expecting to hear the Lord speaking to us personally through it. What reverent concern this will bring!

The second feature to be emphasized in the pattern of these messages is that in all seven cases the Lord begins with the words "I know." To five of the churches He says, "I know thy works"; to Smyrna "I know thy tribulation, and thy poverty"; to Pergamum, "I know where thou dwellest, even where Satan's throne is." Many centuries before, in the time of Israel's bondage in Egypt, the Lord said to Moses, "I know their sorrows; and I am come down to deliver them" (Ex.3:7,8). To the disciples the Lord Jesus said, "Your heavenly Father knoweth that ye have need of all these things" (Matt.6:32). What wealth of comfort is brought to our hearts by the assurance that He understands all our circumstances and is deeply concerned for our welfare. It is also a salutary thing to remember His complete knowledge of all our thoughts and ways. David marvelled at this, as we read in Psalm 139:

"O LORD, Thou has searched me, and known me. Thou knowest my downsitting and mine uprising, Thou understandest my thoughts afar off Thou searchest out my path and my lying down, and art acquainted with all my ways. For there is not a word in my tongue, but, lo, O LORD, Thou knowest it altogether ... Such knowledge is too wonderful for me; it is high, I cannot attain unto it" (Psalm 139:1-4,6).

As David thought of this, he was moved to pray: "Search me, O God, and know my heart: try me, and know my thoughts: and see if there be any way of wickedness in me and lead me in the way everlasting" (vv.23,24). Perhaps from our hearts too this desire will be stirred by the Holy Spirit as we study the letters to the seven churches. When impressed by the Lord's intimate knowledge of motivation, word and deed, we too may invite Him to search our inmost being and reveal anything which would spoil His joy in us or our communion with Him.

A third feature of the Lord's messages to the churches is the Lord's readiness to commend what pleased Him, and His faithfulness in exposing wrong. Usually, He first expressed appreciation of what He could commend before rebuking the disciples for any failures. So typical of our Master! We recognize ourselves to be unprofitable servants at the best. Yet He is so ready to give us credit for our feeble efforts. How thankful also we should feel for His faithfulness in reproof and chastisement; all in perfect love and wisdom, so that we may he partakers of His holiness and serve Him more effectively.

A fourth feature, common to the Lord's message to each church, is the assurance of reward to the overcomer. The overcomer! Mightiest of all overcomers is the Lord Jesus Christ Himself. "I also overcame, and sat down with My Father in His throne" (Rev.3:21). Through all the stress and temptation of His earthly life, including the awful ordeal of suffering at Calvary, the great Captain of our salvation went victoriously forward. As His disciples, you and I must continually battle against the power of the flesh within and the world around. Satan will: do his best to exploit our weaknesses. Christian experience is essentially one of conflict. But thank God we may be more than conquerors through Him who loved us. By the power of the indwelling Spirit of God we are equipped to cope with the daily spiritual pressures, which are the norm for our Christian lives. There is no ground for defeatism. He who is for us is greater than all against us. We are to be strong in the Lord and in the strength of His might. Daily putting on the whole armour of God we shall stand even in the evil day, and having done all, will stand. One day our conflict will be over. Will it be true of you and me, as our life service is reviewed by Christ, that we shall be regarded by Him as overcomers?

The range of reward for the overcomer is immense. We hope to look at some of these as we consider the messages to individual churches. Some of these are difficult for us to understand, for at present we know only in part, seeing as in a glass, darkly. But we recognize each reward promised to be of heavenly distinction and eternal value. Men of this world strive to receive recognition in the special honours to which only few attain in this life. How much more should we be in earnest as spiritual overcomers for Christ, so that in the day of His reward we shall be counted worthy as overcomers. Not of course that we would covet reward for its own sake; rather because the honour of our Lord Jesus Christ will be magnified through our having loved and served Him. In this spirit we may rightly share the apostle Paul's purely motivated spiritual ambition:

> "Forgetting the things which are behind, and stretching forward to the things which are before, I press on toward the goal unto the prize of the high calling of God in Christ Jesus (Phil.3:13,14).

A Christian poet has written these lovely words about the possibility receiving a crown of reward for Christ's hand:

> "The bride eyes not her garment,
> But her dear Bridegroom's face.
> I will not gaze at glory,
> But on my King of grace;
> Not at the crown He giveth,
> But on His pierced hand;
> The Lamb is all the glory
> Of Immanuel's land."

26

THE MESSAGES TO EPHESUS, PERGAMUM AND THYATIRA

EPHESUS

Ephesus is the only one of the seven Asian churches named in Revelation chapters 2 and 3 about which we have any detailed account in the Acts of the Apostles. Paul described the first impact of the gospel in Ephesus as "a great door and effectual" opened by God to him and his fellow-evangelists (1 Cor.16:9). He remained in Ephesus for two years, during which time the Church of God in that city became a powerful centre of testimony - not only in Ephesus itself, but also "all they which dwelt in Asia heard the Word of the Lord, both Jews and Greeks" (Acts 19:10).

Ephesus was a notorious centre of idol worship, with its associated immorality. The city was guardian of the famed temple of Artemis (Diana) and of her image, which was said to have fallen from heaven. So great had been the effect of the gospel that silversmiths who gained their livelihood by making silver shrines of Artemis felt their trade threatened. They stirred up a great riot in protest against the gospel. Yet the work of God prevailed, and the Church in Ephesus was still continuing its testimony as a golden lampstand towards the close of

122

the first century. In the first part of the Lord's message to the disciples in that Church of God he says:

> "These things saith He that holdeth the seven stars in His right hand, He that walketh in the midst of the seven golden lampstands: I know thy works, and thy toil and patience, and that thou canst not bear evil men, and didst try them which call themselves apostles, and they are not, and didst find them false; and thou hast patience and didst bear for My Name's sake, and hast not grown weary" (Rev.2:1-3).

The Lord certainly found many features which were a credit to the disciples in this Ephesian Church - its diligence in spiritual service, its concern to maintain true doctrine, its perseverance and sacrifice. It therefore comes as a surprise to read in verse 4: "But I have this against thee, that thou didst leave thy first love." The Lord not only called on them to repent for this, but solemnly warned them that if they failed to do so the golden lampstand in Ephesus would be removed: that is, they would no longer be recognized by Him as a church of God.

How seriously this reminds us of the importance of motivation in all our service for Christ. Paul could say, "The love of Christ constraineth us". A great deal of activity in spiritual service, perhaps involving much sacrifice, may lose its value to the Lord if it is not done out of love for Him. The point is well made in 1 Corinthians chapter 13: "If I speak with the tongues of men and of angels, but have not love, I am becoming sounding brass, or a clanging cymbal ... and if I bestow all my goods to feed the poor, and if I give my body to be burned, but have not love, it profiteth me nothing" (vv. 1,3).

Indeed, all our service is revitalized when it flows out of our love for Him. Let us seek grace that it may be so, for we should daily be concerned about it. Paul urged the Ephesians to show compassion, kindness, humility and other special graces, but "above all these things put on love". May our hearts share the things of the hymn-writer:

"But though I cannot sing or tell or know
The fulness or Thy love while here below,
My empty vessel I may freely bring;
O Thou, who art of love the living spring,
My vessel fill."

There is something very special to the Lord about our first love - the love which filled our hearts towards Him in the early flow of our conversion and glad commitment to His service. It was the same with His people Israel when they had first been delivered from cruel slavery in Egypt. The point is taken up by Jeremiah: "The word of the LORD came to me, saying, Go, and cry in the ears of Jerusalem, saying, Thus saith the LORD, I remember for thee the kindness of thy youth, the love of thine espousals; how thou wentest after Me in the wilderness, in a land that was not sown" (2:1).

But with many in Israel that warm devotion and love for the Lord quickly grew cold. They became formal in worship and showed dissatisfaction or even rebellion in times of testing. The disciples in Ephesus had also lost their first love. They were still busy and persevering in God's work, but the loving motivation which formerly brought such joy to Him was now lacking. Their service was out of a sense of duty rather than because out of loving hearts they longed to please Him. All this is recorded for our warning and encouragement, lest we too lapse from our first love.

The opposite will be true of us if we are growing in the grace and knowledge of our Lord Jesus Christ. Our love will then deepen and mature. When imprisoned in Rome, Paul was longing for the spiritual progress of the disciples in Philippi, people he loved and knew so well: "God is my witness, how I long after you all in the tender mercies of Christ Jesus. And this I pray, that your love may abound yet more and more in knowledge and all discernment" (1:8,9).

Our love abounding more and more! This is open to every disciple of Christ. It may be brought about through the work of the Holy Spirit who indwells us. For love has precedence in that delightful cluster of virtues described as the "fruit of the Spirit" in Galatians chapter 5: "The fruit of the Spirit is love, joy, peace, longsuffering, kindness, goodness, faithfulness, meekness, temperance" (vv.22, 23). To walk by the Spirit is to walk in love. We are left to wonder how the disciples in Ephesus responded to the Lord's warning and appeal, but the closing words of the Lord's message to them are also for us today: "He that hath an ear; let him hear what the Spirit saith to the Churches. To him that overcometh, to him will I give to eat of the tree of life, which is in the Paradise of God" (2:7).

PERGAMUM AND THYATIRA

The Lord's messages to the Churches in Pergamum and Thyatira contained something to praise and something to criticize, and from it all we can ourselves benefit by way of imitation or warning. The message to Pergamum begins: "These things saith He that hath the sharp two-edged sword: I know where thou dwellest, even where Satan's throne is: and thou holdest fast My Name, and didst not deny My faith, even in the days of Antipas My witness, My faithful one, who was killed among you, where Satan dwelleth (Rev.2:12,13).

So Pergamum is described as the place of Satan's throne and dwelling. Some suggest this may have been expressed in the worship of the Roman Emperor, because a temple had been built in Pergamum in his honour. In many parts of the Roman Empire Christians forfeited their lives rather than give divine honours to the Emperor. Perhaps Antipas, described as the Lord's faithful witness, had been put to death for this reason: typical of many devoted Christians who showed great strength of conviction in following the steps of the Master. Had He not said, 'Whosoever would save his life shall lose it; and whosoever shall lose his life for My sake and the gospel's shall save it'? (Mk.8:35). Living as we do, under less demanding conditions of discipleship, the example of such sacrifice should still challenge our hearts.

> "They met the tyrant's brandished steel,
> The lion's gory mane,
> They bowed their necks the death to feel;
> Who follows in their train?"

Despite such devotion, the Lord had a few things against the Church in Pergamum. Satan had failed to overcome the disciples by violent persecution, so he tried to undermine the Church by subtle corruption through false teaching. "I have a few things against thee", the Lord said, "because thou hast there some that hold the teaching of Balaam" (Rev.2:14). As we learn from the book of Numbers, the teaching of Balaam seduced some of the Israelites to idolatry and its accompanying immorality. If the disciples in Pergamum who had been influenced by this evil failed to repent, the Lord gave warning of prompt action against them: "I will make war against them with the sword of My mouth" (Rev.2:16). This we understand to be the Word of God. We are told in Hebrews that God's Word: "is living and active, and sharper than any two-edged sword, and piercing even to the dividing of soul and spirit, of both joints and marrow, and quick to discern the thoughts and intents of the heart" (Heb.4:12).

When the Lord's message was publicly read to the Church in Pergamum, those who had been secretly sinning would feel its power, recognizing indeed that there is no "creature that is not manifest in His sight: but all things are naked and laid open before the eyes of Him with whom we have to do". Again the Lord offers eternal reward to the overcomer: in this case: "To him ... will I give of the hidden manna, and I will give him a white stone, and upon the stone a new name written, which no one knoweth but he that receiveth it" (Rev.2:17). Doubtless the 'hidden manna' refers back to that placed in a golden pot within the ark of the covenant. In type it speaks of Christ, implying that the overcomer will be granted a special enjoyment of Christ as his portion. A white stone was sometimes given to a victor in the games, so may here speak of the Lord's approval and recognition to a place of authority.

Coming now to the Lord's message to the Church in Thyatira: "These things saith the Son of God, who hath His eyes like a flame of fire and His fret are like unto burnished brass: I know thy works, and thy love and faith and ministry and patience, and that thy last works are more than the first. But I have this against thee, that thou sufferest the woman Jezebel, which calleth herself a prophetess; and she teacheth and seduceth My servants to commit fornication, and to eat things sacrificed to idols."

What a striking contrast the Lord presents between those in Thyatira who earned such a high commendation and others who had yielded to immoral seduction! The Lord evidently held the faithful disciples responsible to take action in purging the Church of this corruption. It was not enough that they kept their own lives pure; moral evil must not be tolerated in others. Paul had to write to the Corinthians about a similar situation. Moral evil had touched the lives of some in the Corinthian Church, but there had been no disciplinary action against them. The apostle commanded that the wicked man should be put away from the Church. In the nature of things, because of our human weaknesses, various evils may creep into the lives of disciples in churches of God. But there is the spiritual authority in those churches to deal with the evil, whether moral or doctrinal. The Lord warned that those in Thyatira who had sinned would be severely punished by Him: "and all the churches shall know that I am He which searcheth the reins and hearts: and I will give unto each one of you according to your works" (Rev.2:23).

Most solemn words! The Psalmist said that holiness becomes God's house for evermore, and in every church of God His standard of holiness must be maintained. "Have no fellowship with the unfruitful works of darkness", Paul urged the Ephesians, "but rather even reprove them" (Eph.5:11). Graciously, the Lord acknowledged those in Thyatira who did not hold to corrupt teaching or practice. They had not learned the called "deep things of Satan." To the Romans Paul wrote: "I would have you wise unto that which is good, and simple unto that which is evil" (Rom.16:19). Far better to remain ignorant of the deep secrets of evil that have the mind stained with things of which it is a shame even to speak. The Lord would lay no greater burden on the faithful in Thyatira. "Howbeit", He said, "that which ye have, hold fast till I come" (Rev.2:25). A word which we also should take to heart. Our Master will not overburden us. His yoke is easy, His burden light. Only let us be faithful to what we have, the truth entrusted to us, the service within our ability. For it is only until He comes:

"A little while, 'twill soon he past!
Why should we shun the shame and Cross?
Oh, let us in His footsteps haste,
And count for Him all else but loss;
Oh, how will recompense His smile
The sufferings of this little while!"

Finally, the Lord encouraged the overcomers in Thyatira: "He that overcometh, and he that keepeth My works unto the end, to him will I give authority over the nations: and he shall rule them with a rod of iron, as the vessels of the potter are broken to shivers; as I also have received of My Father; and I will give him the morning star" (Rev.2:26-28). A promise in line with the great principle that if we suffer with Him we shall also reign with Him. 'Know ye not that the saints shall judge the world?' Paul asked in 1 Corinthians 6:2. There is also the added distinction of receiving from our glorious Lord what is described as 'the morning star' - a special reward at His coming.

27

THE MESSAGES TO SMYRNA, PHILADELPHIA, SARDIS AND LAODICEA

Of the seven Churches to which the Lord Jesus sent the messages recorded in Revelation chapters 2 and 3, there were only two against which He made no specific complaint. The saints in the Churches at Smyrna and Philadelphia were struggling to maintain their witness in the face of strong opposition from what the Lord described as 'synagogues of Satan', composed of 'them which say they are Jews, and they are not' (Rev.2:9).

Doubtless in both cities the local Jewish congregation was in a position to harass disciples of Christ, and in Smyrna even to persecute them with violence. In Romans chapter 2 Paul points out that a person is truly a Jew if he is one inwardly, having known circumcision of the heart. This seems to be behind what the Lord said about those who said they were Jews and were not. Paul had himself been in that position before his conversion to Christ, thinking that he was serving God by persecuting those who loved the Lord Jesus.

For the Churches in both these cities the Lord had a message of encouragement, but with a quite different emphasis. The disciples in Smyrna were to brace themselves for a time of intense persecution, even to martyrdom: those in Philadelphia were to see their adversaries openly put to shame, and fresh

129

opportunity for effective witness would open up to them. Reminding us that the Lord often leads through different paths, calling some to greater suffering than others, yet always supplying the needed grace to match the trial.

To Smyrna the word was given: "I know thy tribulation, and thy poverty, (but thou art rich) ... Fear not the things which thou art about to suffer: behold, the Devil is about to cast some of you into prison, that ye may be tried; and ye shall have tribulation ten days. Be thou faithful unto death, and I will give thee, the crown of life" (Rev.2:9,10). What pleasure it must have given the Lord Jesus to see the reality of faith in this Church! Trial for Christ's sake had reduced them to poverty. Like so many in those times, they had accepted with joy the spoiling of their own possessions by their persecutors. Yet the Lord said they were rich. Reminding us of James 2 verse 5: "Did not God choose them that are poor as to the world to be rich in faith, and heirs to the kingdom which He promised to them that love Him?" Similarly in 2 Corinthians Paul was writing about the trials endured by the apostles in their witness; they were "as chastened, and not killed; as sorrowful, yet always rejoicing; as poor, yet making many rich; as having nothing, and yet possessing all things" (2 Cor.6:9,10). Strange paradox to the natural mind, but true to Christian experience in all generations.

Some in Smyrna would be called upon to yield their lives for Christ. How fitting, then, that the Lord should begin His message by saying: "These things saith the First and the Last, which was dead, and lived again" (Rev.2:8); also that He should promise the crown of life to those who gave their lives for Him; and again that the overcomer would not be hurt at all by the second death. Because Christ died and rose again the believer's eternal life is assured. Death is but the entrance to eternal glory. The second death, that eternal separation under the judgement of God' has no power over those who are Christ's. In addition to this priceless security, there is the promise of the crown of life, a reward for endurance of temptation for those who love their Lord.

The Lord's plan for the Church in Philadelphia seemed to imply less immediate persecution. Those of the synagogue of Satan were to be humbled, and made to know that Christ loved His disciples in that city. The Church had a little power, had kept His Word, and had not denied His Name; they had patiently observed the Master's word. Because they had been uncompromising in principle and loyal in witness for Christ, they were to be kept from the hour of testing which was about to come on the whole world.

Despite the difficulties of the times, the Lord said, "I have set before thee a door opened, which none can shut" (Rev.3:8). Imagine the tonic effect of this promise! At a time which seemed most detrimental to progress, the Lord was promising a fresh opportunity for witness and development. At the conclusion of their first missionary journey, Paul and Barnabas had "rehearsed all things that God had done with them, and how that He had opened a door of faith unto the Gentiles" (Acts 14:27). Paul also wrote of the work in Ephesus, "a great door and effectual is opened unto me" (1 Cor.16:9); and he later asked the Colossians to pray 'that God may open unto us a door for the Word, to speak the mystery of Christ" (Col.4:3). In all our service for Him, how dependent we still are upon the opening of such doors!

There follows a stirring challenge to the Church in Philadelphia: "I come quickly: hold fast that which thou hast, that no one take thy crown" (3:11). Reminding us that the Lord has encouraged every generation of believers to live in expectation of His return. The verse challenges us also with the possibility of forfeiting our crown of reward. If we fail to hold fast what has been entrusted to us, someone else may prove faithful in that very thing, gaining the crown where we have failed. A heart-searching possibility!

Finally, we think of the Lord's promise to the overcomer as He completes His message to Philadelphia: "He that overcometh, I will make him a pillar in the temple of My God, and he shall go out thence no more: and I will write on him the Name of My God and the name of the city of My God, the New Jerusalem, which cometh down out of heaven from My God, and Mine own new Name" (3:12). In the New Jerusalem John saw no temple, for the Lord God Almighty and the Lamb are the temple thereof: which suggests that although there will be no material structure, some who have been faithful disciples of Christ will have a specially close relationship with Deity in that eternal day. They will also be honoured to have placed on them the Lord's own new Name, a Name as yet unknown to us. Wonderful honour indeed!

SARDIS

This book on the Lord's messages to the seven churches of God in Asia (Revelation chapters 2 and 3) concludes with a consideration of the Churches in Sardis and Laodicea. In one sense it is a disappointing finish, because sadly both of these churches were in a poor spiritual condition: nevertheless, there is much we can learn from their experiences. John was instructed to write to the angel of the Church in Sardis:

> "These things saith He that hath ... the seven stars: I know thy works, that thou host a name that thou livest, and thou art dead. Be thou watchful, and establish the things that remain, which were ready to die: for I have found no works of thine fulfilled before My God. Remember therefore how thou host received and didst hear; and keep it, and repent. If therefore thou shalt not watch, I will come as a thief and thou shalt not know what hour I will come upon thee" (Rev.3:1-3).

It is clear that many of the disciples in this Church had lapsed into a lifeless formality. They went through the routine of church activities. They still had the reputation of being an active Church; yet the Lord saw them as dead. In what sense can believers be dead? They have eternal life and are indwelt by the Holy Spirit: these basic facts of their spiritual standing in Christ cannot be changed, but as to fruit-bearing in spiritual experience they may become dead. As Paul wrote to Timothy about widows in the church: "She that is a widow indeed, and desolate, hath her hope set on. God, and continueth in supplications and prayers night and day. But she that giveth herself to pleasure is dead while she liveth" (1 Timothy 5:5,6).

Spiritual life in communion with God is deadened by over-indulgence in pleasure. The Lord's teaching in John chapter 15 also helps us to understand the point: "I am the vine, ye are the branches: he that abideth in Me and I in him, the same beareth much fruit ... If a man abide not in Me, he is cast forth as a branch, and is withered" (vv.5,6). We abide in Christ by keeping His commandments (1 Jn 3:24). As we read the Lord's solemn message to the Church in Sardis we realize how prone we ourselves may be in lapsing into a similar spiritual deadness. The antidote? We must get back to earnest remembrance of truths we received when first we came to Christ and learned of Him; we must obey afresh His Word; we must turn to God in repentance for our failure in the spirit of the Psalmist who prayed: "My soul cleaveth unto the dust: quicken Thou me according to Thy Word" (Ps.119:25).

In spite of the general deadness of the Church in Sardis, a minority brought joy to the Lord's heart: "Thou hast a few names in Sardis which did not defile their garments: and they shall walk with Me in white; for they are worthy. He that overcometh shall thus be arrayed in white garments; and I will in no wise blot his name out of the book of life, and I will confess his name before My Father, and before His angels" (Rev.3:4,5).

The late Mr. John Miller, an outstanding teacher of the Word of God, has commented helpfully on these verses as follows: "Garments speak of habits. Their behaviour was clean. Walking with the lord in unsoiled garments will lead to a closer walk with Him in the ages to come. We must walk with Him in His ways. He will not walk with us in our ways. Enoch and Noah walked with God. Walking with Him demands that there shall be nothing in our lives that causes our hearts to be at a distance from Him." Useful points to ponder!

The overcomer in Sardis was promised that his name would not be blotted out of the book of life, and that the Lord would confess his name before the Father and before the angels. The Lord made a similar promise to those who confess Him before men (Matt.10:32). Strong encouragement for us all as we try to witness for Him in our time!

As to the possibility of a disciple having his name blotted out of the book of life, there would seem to be two different writings. First, in the book of life of the Lamb slain from the foundation of the world, relating to eternal life in Christ (Rev.13:8). Then in the book of life which relates to our service for God, as when Paul writing to the Philippians refers to "my fellow workers whose names are in the book of life" (Rev.4:3). Those redeemed through the blood of the Lamb have their names for ever written in heaven; but as regards the believer's service, failure may result in names being blotted out of God's record.

LAODICEA

Passing now to a consideration of what the Lord had to say to the Church in Laodicea:

> "These things saith the Amen, the faithful and true Witness, the beginning of the creation of God: I know thy works, that thou art neither cold nor hot I would that thou wert cold or hot. So because thou art lukewarm, and neither hot nor cold, I will spew thee out of My mouth. Because thou sayest, I am rich, and have gotten riches and have need of nothing; and knowest not that thou art the wretched one and miserable and poor and blind and naked I counsel thee to buy of Me gold refined by fire, that thou mayest become rich; and white garments, that thou mayest clothe thyself and that the shame of thy nakedness be not made manifest; and eyesalve to anoint thine eyes, that thou mayest see" (Rev.3:14-18).

This is the most scathing rebuke among all the Lord's messages to the seven churches. Nothing to commend; not a single word of appreciation: only the spelling out of the Laodiceans' incredible self-satisfaction, their unawareness of their true state in the sight of their Lord. How blind at times we also may be to our true spiritual state as He assesses us! At the heart of the problem in Laodicea seemed to be their material affluence. They had lost a sense of true values. Imagine any Christian daring to say, "I ... have need of nothing"! Someone has described Laodicea as the Church with no need for a prayer meeting! If it had been left to us we might well have written off the Church in Laodicea as beyond recovery. But not so with our gracious Master. He assures those in the Church: "As many as I love, I reprove and chasten: be zealous therefore; and repent. Behold, I stand at the door and knock: if any man hear My voice and open the door, I will come in to him, and will sup with him, and he with Me" (Rev.3:19,20).

The Lord had been slighted and ignored by the attitude of the Laodiceans. But He gave them opportunity to have renewed fellowship with Him. Still today, He stands at our heart's door, we who are His disciples. He longs for us to have communion with Him. But He will not force an entrance. We must invite Him in. The spiritual fellowship will be renewed, the joy of our salvation restored. The Master's final word to the Laodiceans contains' the promise: "He that overcometh, I will give to him to sit down with Me in My throne, as I also overcame, and sat down with My Father in His throne. He that hath an ear, let him hear what the Spirit saith to the churches" (Rev.3:21,22).

ABOUT THE PUBLISHER

Hayes Press (www.hayespress.org) is a registered charity in the United Kingdom, whose primary mission is to disseminate the Word of God, mainly through literature. It is one of the largest distributors of gospel tracts and leaflets in the United Kingdom, with over 100 titles and many thousands dispatched annually. In addition to paperbacks and eBooks, Hayes Press also publishes Plus Eagles' Wings, a fun and educational Bible magazine for children, and Golden Bells, a popular daily Bible reading calendar in wall or desk formats.

If you would like to contact Hayes Press, there are a number of ways you can do so:

By mail:c/o The Barn, Flaxlands, Royal Wootton Bassett, Wiltshire, UK SN4 8DY

By phone: 01793 850598

By eMail:info@hayespress.org

via Facebook: www.facebook.com/hayespress.org

MORE BOOKS ON BIBLE PROPHECY

THE FINGER OF PROPHECY

Are you fascinated by the subject of Bible prophecy and the end times that is contained in the Books of Revelation, Daniel, Ezekiel and others? Are you looking for Bible prophecy to be explained, including the keys to understanding prophetic imagery? In this comprehensive Bible commentary, you will find Bible Prophecy 101 as well as 102 and 103! Two Bible teachers combine to give a comprehensive overview of what the Bible has to say about the future - this would be an ideal companion to an in-depth prophecy bible study as well as an excellent overview of the subject for the beginner.

1. The Certainty of Prophecy
2. The Lord's Coming to the Air
3. The Judgement Seat of Christ
4. The Marriage of the Lamb
5. The Times of the Gentiles
6. The Gathering of Israel
7. Final Grouping and Leadership of the Nations
8. The Great Tribulation
9. The Elect of Those Days
10. The Battle of Armageddon
11. The Coming of the Son of Man
12. The Judgement Seat of Christ
13. The Millennial Reign
14. The Great White Throne Judgement

15. Unto the Ages of the Ages

Appendices:

- Old Testament Prophecies

- New Heaven and New Earth

- What is the City of Revelation 21:9 to 22:5?

- Suggested layout of the holy district as shown to Ezekiel

THE FUTURE IN BIBLE PROPHECY

Current world events are making people wonder what the future holds. Are you looking for Bible prophecy to be explained in an interesting and informative way? Brian Johnston provides some key principles for unlocking the meaning of Bible prophecy and surveys what the Bible says about the future, primarily from the books of Daniel and Revelation. Topics covered include: – Will there ever be a United States of Europe? – Will there be a single world currency? – What is the critical position of Israel in God's purposes? – Will the temple be rebuilt in Jerusalem? – What can we know about the Antichrist? – Will Jesus Christ return once, or twice? – What is the role of Babylon in the end times? – What is the significance of the spread of Islam and the rise of ISIS?

THE NATIONS OF THE OLD TESTAMENT: THEIR RELATIONSHIP WITH ISRAEL AND BIBLE PROPHECY

Enhance your understanding of the Old Testament with this helpful introduction to many of the major nations mentioned, with a particular focus on their relationship with Israel and their place in Bible prophecy: The Phoenicians, The Ammonites, The Moabites, The Edomites, The Philistines, The Egyptians, The Ethiopians, The Assyrians, The Syrians, The Babylonians, The Medes and Persians, The Gibeonites, The Rechabites , The Rechahites

A STUDY IN PROPHETIC PRINCIPLES

Do you find Bible prophecy to be a confusing subject? Would you like to be able to understand Bible prophecy about the end times, not just in the book of Revelation, but in the Bible books of Daniel, Ezekiel and others as well? In this concise Bible commentary, George Prasher, Bible teacher and missionary, provides the keys to Bible prophecy by exploring and explaining the underlying principles and patterns in four main sections:

1. The significance and range of prophecy in the plan of divine revelation
2. Patterns of prophetic presentation
3. The main themes of Bible prophecy
4. A study of false prophecy

www.ingramcontent.com/pod-product-compliance
Lightning Source LLC
Chambersburg PA
CBHW071333150726
47997CB00002B/708